A Virtue of

Disobedience

Asim Qureshi

First published in the United Kingdom 27th April 2018 by:

First Edition

ISBN: 978-1-912395-04-0

In the Name of Allāh, the Most Beneficent, the Most Merciful.

Dedication

To my mentor, Dr Scharlette Holdman, who we also knew as Aunty Asma, and who my children called Dado. You helped me to find the human being behind the offence, to see past and through all the noise. Your loss to us all is incalculable. To save the life of one is to save humanity, and you exemplified how humanity, and our inner humanity can be saved one person at a time.

Asim Qureshi

Contents

A Virtue of Disobedience

We are the disobedient look upon us and despair
for we outlast history, time and memory
we are always there.
We are the unquenchable thirst for justice
the bodies that do not bend
tongues you cannot straightjacket
and eyes that will not be turned blind.
We are the step you trip on in the night
the nightmare you wake from but cannot recall
the lump under the rolling hill that reminds you what
is buried there.
We are the disobedient.
We bear witness and we testify.
We love despite the lie that we are not worthy
We hold despite being told we should hide.
Yes; we are the disobedient
who refuse to die
for bodies without eulogies
will never remain in their graves
we are the ghosts of the unmourned
and the spirit of the never grieved.
We are the original traitors to the tireless tyrant
We are Muḥammad
We are Malcolm
We are Moses and Assata
We are Toussaint and Bhashani
We are Rosa and Rabbani
We are the disobedient.
Truth speakers with tongues of fire

Knowledge seekers who provoke your ire
Mouths always moist from sincere prayer.
We are hearts beating for the truth
not like fluttering birds in cages
but like the earth in her final convulsions
like mountains when they scatter to dust
We dismantle, uproot, expose.
We are the disobedient
and we have come not to claim what is yours
but what is and always was ours:
our humanity.
But no - not claim
for it was always with us
and our announcement of that
is the blasphemy you burn us for.
But there's a reason you mustn't play with fire
because flames are not bound by only your aims
if you burn our bodies in the morning
the fire will be licking your heels that night.
Do you feel secure then?
When we are bound not by law but justice?
Loyal not to pen marks on paper but truth?
We are unconquerable and unmanageable
because you can take what you want
if all you want is to take.
We are your greatest fear: fearless
loyal not even to life.
There is no bargain to be made then
for disruption is our only security

in a world which says that security is ensured only
through our repression
- what basis has such authority to be obeyed?
No; we are the disobedient
who refuse to know our place
undivided, low, and mighty
we are a
a unity, a community,
a principle above place.
We are the disobedient.
We declare the emperor naked
and don't kneel before the queen
we smash the idols
confront the Pharaoh
upend the fabric of the world
we will not sell our souls for hallowed halls
we cannot be unmoved
We are the disobedient
we exceed the boundaries
overspill and overspeak.
We are unboxed, unharnessed, unfathomable
unpalatable
uncompromising.
Oh Ozymandiases of the world
do you really think yourselves kings of kings?
How quickly you forget.
Nothing outlasts the fading of the day
but the light of truth itself?

Suhaiymah Manzoor-Khan

Illuminating the Heavens

Asim - 1 - Qureshi

"Truth, she thought. As terrible as death. But harder to find."
[Philip K Dick – The Man in the High Castle]

"Clichés became cliches for a reason; that they usually hold at least a modicum of truth, and the following cliché is truer than most: You can't know where you're going if you don't know where you've been."
[William Gibson – Neuromancer]

"It made her sad, thinking about the consequences of their anger, their thirst for revenge. Her husband was gone, ripped from her, and for what? People were dying, and for what? She thought how things could've gone so differently, how they'd had all these dreams, unrealistic perhaps, of a real change in power, an easy fix to impossible and intractable problems. Back then she'd been unfairly treated, but at least she'd been safe. There had been injustice, but she'd been in love. Did that make it okay? Which sacrifice made more sense?"
[Hugh Howey – Wool]

I am left wondering where to go next.

It is the reason I started writing this book, really first for myself, and also perhaps for my children. There is a cacophony of voices and sounds that deafen the mind. Technology and the speed with which I am able to access billions of megabytes of useless information distracts my soul. This moment can only be described as stagnation.

It has now been fourteen years since I first actively began to engage in a process of holding the state to account in partnership and in service to the communities that I seek to assist - primarily through the organisation CAGE, of whom I have been a member for most of my active life. I am left wondering about the efficacy of my efforts during that time...what did we achieve...and was there ever any point in it?

My detractors, particularly in the political class and the media, claim that I am actually part of the problem, that rather having spent the entirety of my working life in the service of others, I have instead aided the cause of those who wish to cause harm. My heart tells me this is not the case, but my heart is also a human heart and it cannot sometimes hear above the din of what is being projected at it. It is tough when the state seeks to undermine you.

This is not a manifesto. It is not some magnum opus that I feel will move mountains and bring an end to tyrannical and despotic regimes. It is a culmination of my thoughts, feelings and reflections as I have sought to rethink my relationship with my work, and I hope that these thoughts will have some degree of benefit for those who come after me.I also want to make it clear that this is not a doctrinal discussion – for there are scholars who working on these issues who can provide more clear and accurate guidance. But as a researcher who has spent his entire working life in the field, there are reflections that I would like to share for my own thinking and for the sake of our communities. I hope that this is a start of a conversation between Muslims, and also those outside of Islam who perhaps may have their own contributions to make to this discussion.

My sons. I hope you will read these words one day and find that they help you to confront whatever world you find yourself in. This book may end up seeming a contradiction to you. Surely your mother and I have always taught you to be obedient and respectful to your elders, to your teachers, to all those around you who have a collective care for you? Yet here I am...thinking about how disobedience might be a thing of virtue. Be just, and bear witness to Allāh (God), even if it is against yourself. These (paraphrased) words of Allāh from the Qur'ān have formed the centrepiece of my thinking, and so now I will attempt to turn back to them in order to reorganise my thoughts in a way that is necessary for me, and I pray beneficial to you.

With long pieces that I write, I often do not write the introduction until the end...for what can I really say about something that I don't really know I am going to say yet? I want you as the reader to know that as I write this, I'm on a journey of my own, and so I begin with my thoughts on why I began this, in the hope that something true will emerge by the end. Currently, I just know the feeling that I have in my heart, and that is one that is dissatisfied with the status quo - and so I write. This is a process of tafakkur and tadabbur, of contemplation and pondering – of both my religion and my politics – and the pseudo-sabbatical I have taken from my work has been very much with this contemplation in mind. As ibn al-Qayyim al-Jawziyya said:

> *Contemplation necessitates the unveiling (inkishaf) of matters and the manifestation of their realities. It differentiates their degrees of*

goodness and evilness, allows one to recognize the causes that lead to or prevent their occurrence, as well as what hinders their requisites from manifesting.[i]

I have seen 'exceptional' legislation and policy become further entrenched within the country we call home, a place that owns a great part of my identity...my damned urge to queue for instance. I have seen my country lose its sense of self and identity, or perhaps I was mistaken all along and it never existed? Perhaps the emperor is finally wearing his new clothes, and I need to resign myself to the notion that there is no going back, that we cannot restore a balance, that inequity and prejudice will always be the norm? I do not have those answers yet, for I am only just starting this journey, but I pray to Allāh that whatever I find coming out of the other end of this book, is the courage to say what is right, and to have a heart full of love and hope. Any other result would perhaps destroy my resolve.

I very much hope that those outside of the 'House of Islam' will be able to relate to this book. I am writing it as a Muslim, in many ways for Muslims, but then I have always held that certain notions of justice are transcendental, and so perhaps there will be something useful from inside Islam for those outside. It is always an honour and privilege to be able to share one's faith and reflections on faith with a wider audience. I want to be disobedient to the power of the state when it immorally encroaches. Note, I did not say illegally, as there is much that may be legal yet immoral vis-a-vis the Third Reich. When I see friends, those I love, and those I dislike, being directly impacted by national security policies, it drives my spirit towards resistance.

Yet, when I sit in the jumma khutba (the Friday prayer sermon) my local Imam tells me that one day of anarchy is worse than a thousand years of injustice. He further explains that we have a duty of obedience to the leader, and the institutions that help the leader maintain order including the police. I'll be honest, I didn't have much problem with most of what he was saying, until he said, even if he oppresses you, you should not protest against it, as protesting leads to anarchy and is disbelief – just look at the Arab Spring. I think I have found the voice of my virtuous disobedience here. The Imam, in a bizarre way, has convinced me of the need for thoughtfulness around active disobedience. A disobedience that is rooted in scripture and praised for its conscionability.

As I write these words...this entire conversation takes on a new meaning. In four hours I will support my colleague Muhammad Rabbani who is scheduled to appear at the police station in order to learn if he will be charged with a crime for refusing to give the UK police the passwords to his devices when he was stopped at Heathrow. By refusing to give the keys to his digital world, he is protecting crucial evidence from a torture victim that implicates a high profile figure. Not only that, he is standing up for the privacy of us all.

I will write about his courage and principle later, but this is a man who has exemplified in action, the disobedience I seek to understand and convey. This is real; Rabbani has chosen to actively disobey the law based on his conscience, as Rosa Parks chose to disobey a law based on hers – he has chosen to place principle above his own liberty.

Having spent hours speaking to him, it is clear in my mind about one thing: the righteousness of his actions stem from his religious and moral convictions. Our work at the advocacy organisation CAGE has taught us that we must place principle over liberty – in fact we had been discussing this very point in the months prior to his arrest. After that we were given the opportunity to show what principle really looks like in action.

In the case of this work, my aim is to desecularise the notion of action from spirit. As a Muslim, who is conscious of Allāh, I want to place my social justice commitments within the circulatory system of my spirituality - I don't want to 'punch-out' at the end of my activism day and 'punch-in' to the mosque for my spirit – for if there is no connection between the two then how can I still understand being a Muslim in a world that is full of injustice, particularly when millions of those I share a connection with are the subjects of that oppression?

Finally, this is a conversation. I hope that if people honour me with time to read this book, that they will think to meet with me and write to me in order to engage with the ideas I am presenting. My parents taught me that kind manners and good behaviour are prerequisites to being a good Muslim. These are characteristics I am trying to pass on to my children (however badly). What I also want to give them (which perhaps also came from my father specifically) is the idea that you can be surrounded by complete darkness and all alone, but that inside us flickers a flame that when given the oxygen of truth, is capable of illuminating the heavens.

Time and Trauma

"Time's the thief of memory"
[Stephen King – The Gunslinger]

"All children have to be deceived if they are to grow up without trauma."
[Kazuo Ishiguro – Never Let Me Go]

"It takes ten times as long to put yourself back together as it does to fall apart."
[Suzanne Collins – Mockingjay]

For this Muslim...time has meaning.

It is sometimes difficult for us to conceive of time, as we do not live our lives constantly in a state of self-reflection. Our daily activities and anxieties preoccupy our minds, creating an internal chasm in which we are not able to hear or see anything beyond the immediacy of our concerns. This pseudo-reality constricts rather than liberates us. We become infatuated with the bright lights and distinct sounds. For most, the world is a paradise filled with opportunity and desire. For the one who reflects, it can be a prison.

'Time' in the Qur'ān is referenced at one point as al-Asr, leaving the impression of the 'fading day'[ii] – the light that has almost been extinguished, and with it the prospect of activity, progression or movement towards something positive.

I want to think about time. I want to reflect on it so I appreciate its significance and know better how it applies to me. When I ask myself what thirteen years of my life means, it leads me to reflect on the years between 2002 until 2015.

Now, let us eviscerate those years, pretend, for a moment, they never existed. I want to remove from our minds the culmination of experiences, achievements or failures of those years. Send into a black hole the embraces of those you loved – for they no longer exist. Imagine they no longer played a role in shaping the person you are today. Ask yourself: what is the significance, precisely, of the loss of those years from your life?

For me it means that I was never married to my wife. It means that none of my three boys would have existed - that I would never have witnessed them developing through all the small and large stages of their childhood. It would mean that I would never have graduated from my law degree, or my masters. I would never travelled large parts of the world, written a book or had the opportunity to meet my heroes, the survivors of terrible violations who resist being victims of their abuse.

It is these years...these thirteen years that were stolen from the released Guantanamo Bay detainee, Shaker Aamer, now home with his British family in the UK. Aamer lost that entire period of time due to his unlawful kidnapping by the US. He was deprived of a life that might have otherwise been lived.

For many who think about the impact of arbitrary or incommunicado detention, often there is a perception that it is the detention or torture that is the real violation, and that release results in an end to the atrocity. But nothing could be further from the truth, for nothing can replace the time that has been lost.

How does Shaker Aamer get back the years of relationship building with his children, the youngest he met for the first time when he was released? How does he, and how do his children, integrate an emotional connection that they were deprived of that entire time? We can try to understand:

> *As has been widely reported, Aamer was afraid to meet his kids, these adolescent strangers, how he rushed to hug them, but not they him, how he told them they could not expect to love him right away after such an absence. "I want you to know I did not leave you. We were forcefully separated. I do not want you to blame me or your mother."*

> *To keep himself sane – sometimes in solitary confinement, always in discomfort, often in pain – he befriended ants and other insects, gave them names. Aamer fed birds, much as he did as a child: it takes patience. Throughout his detention he was denied his normal toothpick to clean his teeth but kept the stem of his daily*

> *apple to do the job, despite efforts to take it*
> *away. This is part of how prisoners keep their*
> *dignity. It's worse, we can all imagine, if you're*
> *innocent.[iii]*

Speaking to another released detainee who had been kept away from his family for three years, I asked him how he built a relationship with his youngest child, who he only met after release. The heart breaking response I received was that this released detainee only managed to hug his child with the full emotional connection much later.

The long lasting and deep impact of trauma that results from unlawful detention cannot simply be reduced to imprisonment and release, as the loss of time and connection results in devastating consequences that are difficult for us to fully comprehend.

But I forget. I have been so focused on individuals who have been harmed, that I forget that their detention is like throwing a grenade into their communities. The consequences are devastating for the immediate family but our family structures are so much wider than parents, siblings, spouses or children. Families that once enjoyed economic prosperity find themselves in poverty. Those on the path of education find themselves falling away. For communities, the impacts are so wide reaching that they are difficult to capture. Looking at the US, I am reminded of the devastating impact that mass incarceration of black men has had. As Michelle Alexander tells us in 'The New Jim Crow', this is not just about AWOL fathers, but about how one in three black men will at some point be incarcerated:

> *Hundreds of thousands of black men are unable*
> *to be good fathers for their children, not because*
> *of a lack of commitment or desire but because*

they are warehoused in prisons, locked in cages. They did not walk out on their families voluntarily; they were taken away in handcuffs, often due to a massive federal program known as the War on Drugs.[iv]

From the community, while some will stand with the family of those unlawfully detained, many will choose to ostracise.[v] This is not due to their belief that the family are terrorists or that individuals still pose a threat, but they are understandably acting to protect their own from similar types of harm. They want to avoid guilt by association. This response, aided by an alarmist media, is destructive in the long term. Almost self cannibalistic, it subverts the very notion of community, of togetherness, of umma (something I will return to later).

For those who are not directly affected by what Agamben termed the 'state of exception'[vi], it is difficult for them to conceive of the harm that is caused by this exceptional state. The wider population is told that whatever is being done, is necessary and proportional to the threat of terrorism, and yet they are not the ones to suffer the consequences of those violent policies, for it is a form of violence to 'exceptionalise' families and communities.

For someone like former UK Prime Minister Tony Blair, the suggestion of 90 days pre-charge detention being a proportionate response was risible – for he will never experience its impact. We will be told by others (mostly liberals) that Tony Blair was defeated – the House of Commons successfully managed to negotiate the 90 days pre-charge detention down to 28 days and congratulated themselves on their success. Yet what does 28 days mean to them?

We must remember, that a month being held without charge or trial does not exist without consequence, the repercussions are great, for when the home is raided:

- The individual under suspicion is frightened by the violent entry of the police.
- The spouse and children are terrorised by the state's intrusion into the sleeping hours of their home.
- The large number of police cars and vans creates a spectacle of fear in the area.
- The neighbours become suspicious of the family.
- Friends and family question whether assisting the individual and their family will bring them under suspicion.
- The individual is named and shamed in the national press – before any charges have been brought.
- The employer of the individual must deal with the negative media around the individual, but further make a decision about whether to continue to employ the person due to the 28 days absence. In most cases the individual is fired.

According to UK government statistics, between 2016-2017, only 4% of those arrested due to suspicion of terrorism, were charged with terrorism offences – that is 15 people out of 379.[vii] One must also remember, that when terrorism charges do take place, they are nearly always for non-violent offences, there is never a violent plot or act involved. Even if the majority of those arrested are never charged, the reality is that media coverage of the arrest can be just as devastating to lives of those affected as any charge may have had.

On top of the trauma of raids, the quagmire of fear-based narratives about Muslims and Islam have a profoundly negative impact. For those Muslims growing up in the 70s, 80s and 90s, there are parts of public life that were troubling and problematic, but largely it was something that could be understood within wider narratives around privilege, class, race and so on.

But today, there is an entire generation of young Muslims – those who were younger than sixteen when the World Trade Centre attack of 2001 took place - that have only ever known a political reality where they are labelled as being potential future threats. This takes place across multiple platforms, from children in the school calling Muslim pupils 'terrorists' as a form of bullying[viii], to teachers implementing the duty imposed by the counter-terrorism policy Prevent within schools, to politicians speaking about Muslims as outsiders[ix], to the conversation about Britain and finally, of course, to the way in which the media presents those narratives.

For the average Muslim child, they are drip-fed a narrative on a daily basis that they are to be feared. If not now, then potentially in the future.

Since 9/11, those under sixteen have only ever known this world. For them there has been no other political reality to hail, for as far as they are concerned, they have always been a 'problem'. When this mirror is held up over a period of time, the result on the individual and collective psyche is extremely damaging. I am deeply concerned about the long term impacts of this situation on communities, and I question the extent to which patiently waiting through it is an actual solution to the problems we face. This is particularly so when I turn to the experience of those in Ireland. As for a former trustee of the British charity British Irish Rights Watch (now Rights Watch UK), my role on the board was to very much think of the cross-fertilisation of policy and experience between Ireland and the War on Terror – a thinking exercise that often resulted in powerful similarities.

The adage 'time heals all wounds' is often invoked as a form of pseudo-psychology to assist those who have suffered a traumatic experience or lived through some difficulty to come to terms with their suffering. This linear conception of trauma and time, however, somewhat betrays their cyclical nature, and the way that trauma can potentially manifest itself continually throughout generations.

The next generation I spoke about above, are living through times when all sorts of the markers are being left on their psychology and physiology – markers that we have begun to understand through the link between trauma and epigenetics. Studies show that in mammals, environmental factors leave markers on transgenes, which are then transmitted between generations – in the other words, trauma travels.[x] It is important for us to understand the way in which this trauma manifests itself, not only in the present, but also across generations. Hala Alyan captures the pain of how trauma follows Palestinian families from the Nakba (1948 Catastrophe) into the diaspora in her novel 'Salt Houses':

> *"Allāh have mercy, she has your brother's blood in her."*
>
> *Across the room Alia winced, watching her daughter, all those likenesses, those hurts— scrawled plainly on her pretty face. Mustafa, whose name they go entire years at a time without speaking. It became a tacit rule between her and Atef: If it hurts, leave it. Their marriage had a glove compartment, a hollow, cluttered space where emotional debris went— Mustafa, those first months in Kuwait, Nablus. Palestine tossed in there like an illegible receipt, keys that no longer opened any door. Why would we, Atef seemed to beg her silently in*

*those early years after the war, his face
tightening with pain when she spoke of Nablus,
when she cursed Meir and Rabin and the day
they'd been born. So she spoke of it less and less,
everything they'd left behind, her dreams of
walking into her childhood bedroom, the way
her entire body drummed when she thought of
the place that was, suddenly, not hers anymore.
She folded it away.[xi]*

This is not an experience that is unknown. It is
familiar to many who have suffered, and then went on
to make others suffer. S. Yizhar (real name Yizhar
Smilansky) wrote his account of life as a soldier in a
fictional novella, set during the Nakba in May 1949, one
year after the first expulsion of the Palestinians. The
account by Yizhar is remarkable, because it provides an
insight into the thoughts and feelings of a Zionist
soldier, who has heard the stories and understood the
two thousand years of oppression of the Jews. Unlike
his comrades, he finds the human being inside himself
who goes further than limiting his own personal and
community's trauma's to their experience, and in a
remarkable act of empathy superimposes that trauma
on to the plight of his victims:

*Exalted in their pain and sorrow above our—
wicked—existence they went on their way and
we could also see how something was
happening in the heart of the boy, something
that, when he grew up, could only become a
viper inside him, that same thing that was now
the weeping of a helpless child.*

*Something struck me like lightning. All at once
everything seemed to mean something different,
more precisely: exile. This was exile. This was
what exile was like. This was what exile looked
like.*

> *I couldn't stay where I was. The place itself couldn't bear me. I went round to the other side. There the blind people were sitting. I hastily skirted round them. I went through the gap into the field that was bounded by the cactus hedge. Things were piling up inside me.*
>
> *I had never been in the Diaspora—I said to myself— I had never known what it was like... but people had spoken to me, told me, taught me, and repeatedly recited to me, from every direction, in books and newspapers, everywhere: exile. They had played on all my nerves. Our nation's protest to the world: exile! It had entered me[...]*[xii]

Trauma creates vipers in the heart...I think our contemporary world has born witness to this one truth more than any other.

Throughout this chapter I have attempted to describe the ways in which a securitised narrative around a community as a scatter-gun policy can have wide-reaching and devastating consequences. This is significant, as we attempt to understand how individual trauma and the passage of time converge to harm. On the onset of a traumatic experience, the amygdala and hippocampus operate to assist the body in its fight or flight response by flooding the body with much needed adrenaline in order to protect itself. The state that emerges is known as 'arousal' or 'hyper-arousal', allowing the body to be at the maximum heightened sense of alertness necessary to evade harm. This process happens on a day by day basis to most people, but the body is able to regulate the state between arousal and normality much better due to the lack of extremes between the two positions.

A significantly traumatic incident, such as police brutality, torture, rape or living under the threat of bombing, results in a heightened state of arousal that then becomes a permanent feature of the affected individual's life. For some, after release from prison, the sound of keys clinking in a completely normal environment, will force the body to enter the state of arousal, re-experiencing the fear of the previous trauma, as the sound of keys clinking in prison was previously indicative of a torture session that was soon to begin. Often the affected person will not know they are in the state of arousal, and this can lead to complications in his/her relationships, as others cannot understand how or why the mundanity of normal life could lead to extreme responses. I am reminded of one of my heroes, Gerry Conlan, who suffered greatly as an incarcerated innocent man, who was tortured into confessing his involvement in the 1974 Guildford bomb plot. After his release, Gerry was devastated by his experience, resulting in alcoholism and drug addiction, as well as a number of suicide attempts – despite his activism for the rights of others.[xiii] It is a stark reminder to me that the survivors, despite their heroism in combatting the very thing they suffered, continue to be haunted by demons that are often unseen.

I also recall meeting with one family who had escaped a difficult conflict and bombing campaign. On speaking to the father of the family as to whether or not he had witnessed the signs of any trauma on their exit to safety, he was adamant that he had seen no such thing. I knew that the family had lived through some heavy shelling and seen some horrible things on their route to refuge, so did not believe that the father knew what to look for. Changing track, I asked a simple question: "What happens in your house when someone bangs the door shut too loudly?" The father started laughing at this, saying how it was funny that they would all jump more than normal and that his daughter would go and hide under a table – he saw this as some kind of amusing post-safety activity, not realising that his entire family's bodies were responding to previous trauma, and attempting to save themselves, even in an environment of safety and security. When I explained the processes of the body in response to these sounds, he finally understood that they would need the help of a trauma specialist to assist them back to safety and normality.

The trauma is never-ending, in fact, in the context of conflict it is self-perpetuating but perhaps meaningfully so? The French philosopher Gregoire Chamayou, in commenting on this seemingly never-ending cycle said:

> ...the objection that drone strikes are counterproductive because they allow the enemy, in a classic pattern of action and repression, to recruit more volunteers no longer applies. Never mind if the enemy ranks thicken, since it will always be possible to neutralize the new recruits as fast as they emerge. The cull will be repeated periodically, in a pattern of infinite eradication. Once antiterrorism, overtakes counterinsurgency, we are led to understand, the sufficient aim becomes a regular elimination of emerging threats, which takes the form of a periodic reaping: "Kill enough of them and the threat goes away.. .. However, the 'kill list'.... never gets shorter, the names and faces are simply replaced." Caught up in an endless spiral, the eradication strategy is, paradoxically, destined never to eradicate. The very dynamics of its perverse effects prevent it from ever fully decapitating a hydra that regenerates itself ceaselessly as a result of the strategy's own negativity.[xiv]

Stories of trauma travel. They cannot help but do so.

Often stories are communicated both horizontally, so they reinforce narratives of contemporaries, but often they travel vertically, creating both history and mythology. They travel down through the generations, so young Jewish children are told of the atrocities perpetrated against their grandparents and great grandparents through the pogroms and the Holocaust, and young Palestinian children are told of the atrocities perpetrated against their parents and grandparents since the Nakba.

We now know that what is related through the written word and the tongue is internalised by those who identify with the struggle. But there is a story that travels through the veins, through the very DNA of each generation. Through the science of epigenetics, we know that traumatic instances leave a genetic mark, one that travels to the next generation. Is this where we can begin to understand the cyclical nature of violence? That as sides of a conflict increasingly resort to barbarity in their conduct, so future generations are destined to be impacted genetically by the choices that are made in the past.

On its own, the movement of time is not a healer.

Within the Islamic tradition, I see something ever present in the Qur'ān and the teachings of the Prophet Muḥammad (peace and blessings be upon him): a view to the past that informs the present. The significance of this for me is shown in the fact that almost a third of the Qur'ān is the stories of past nations. With this comes the constant reminder that a backwards glance at history is not just an act of storytelling, but a direct huda or guidance in the life of the Muslim. History, as an aspect of time, is not just relegated to the past, but according to the Qur'ān informs the present:

> *Do people think that they will be left to say 'We believe' without being put to the test? We tested*

> *those who went before them: God will certainly*
> *mark out which ones are truthful and which*
> *ones are lying.[xv]*

I am struck by these verses that do not appear just once, but are often repeated in the Qur'ān. In the second chapter, al-Baqarah, a similar formulation is given by Allāh: that until we are tested with a test like the people of the past, then we should not expect to enter Paradise. Some of these tests are described, such as poverty, hardship and natural disasters, being indicative of the difficulties that human beings face, whether large or small.

Reading an introductory book to Catholic Liberation Theology in the context of Latin America, I find similar ideas about the text being linked to understanding the context of oppression in the contemporary world:

> *Liberative hermeutics reads the Bible as a book*
> *of life, not as a book of strange stories. The*
> *textual meaning is indeed sought, but only as a*
> *function of the practical meaning: the*
> *important this is not so much interpreting the*
> *text of the scriptures as interpreting life*
> *"according to the scriptures." Ultimately, this*
> *old/new reading aims to find contemporary*
> *actualization (practicality) for the textual*
> *meaning.[xvi]*

If the Qur'ān itself places so much importance on history, then to my mind, it cannot be the only history that we can learn from. It must mean that the culminated experiences of civilisations and societies open themselves up for reflection. This is an active process that must constantly take place. For us to learn as humanity, a constant referencing and reframing of the contemporary in relation to the past must occur.

One example is how commentators have, ad nauseam, analysed the rhetoric and propaganda emanating from President Donald Trump's administration in its own right, but the more astute hear the echoes of the Nazis – simply because history teaches.

Travelling around the world to meet with detainees released from prison, I listened as they told me how they had studied at jamiat Yusu for the University of Joseph - the Abrahamic Prophet detained in Egypt according to the Qur'ān.These detained men find solace in historical references, past stories that echo their own.

A recent book that exemplifies this Qur'ānic guidance for the Muslim is 'On Tyranny: Twenty Lessons from the Twentieth Century' by the American writer Timothy Snyder. By focusing on the past, and directly extracting lessons from it, Snyder is able to encapsulate the significance of reflecting on history as a means of instruction:

> *We might be tempted to think that our democratic heritage automatically protects us from such threats. This is a misguided reflex. Our own tradition demands that we examine history to understand the deep sources of tyranny, and to consider the proper responses to it. We are no wiser than the Europeans who saw democracy yield to fascism, Nazism, or communism in the twentieth century. Our one advantage is that we might learn from their experience. Now is a good time to do so.[xvii]*

As perfectly described by Snyder, the backwards glance at history instructs us by being able to determine modalities of oppression and repression. But this glancing also provides us with exemplars of resistance.

As the adage tells us, there is nothing new under the sun. With that in mind, I seek to understand what it means to be a Muslim who is disobedient to oppression, and how that disobedience forms part of the necessary aspects of spiritual and civic life. I want to learn from those who came before me, from the heroic Sufis like Imam Shamil in Chechnya and Omar Mukhtar in Libya. I want to understand how Abu Hanifa and ibn Taymiyya confronted authority. I wish to glean from Malcolm X and Martin Luther King Jr the hidden secrets of resisting the State, when the weight of the state comes to bear down on you with repressive policies. I hope that by communing with Steve Biko, Nelson Mandela and Walter Sisulu, I will get some answers to how a heart full of principle, in a void filled with hate, can survive.

The ghosts of the past speak through pages that I read. They bear testament to their struggles, but as I read them, they also bear testament to ours. In matters of injustice, time stops. Common understandings of injustice can be picked up and placed in almost any circumstance anywhere in the world and in any time period – in a way they lose their temporality, as modalities often do not change.

The consequences of the injustice, however, echo. They reverberate in the hearts of men, women and children who take on the status of bystanders, victims or survivors. The only one who truly survives, is the one who resists this time defying injury, the one who is disobedient to injustice.

The Cycles of Iblis, Exodus and Oppression

Asim - 31 - Qureshi

"...free phones from a state-run telecom company turn out to have been a Trojan horse when citizens discover that their private conversations are being transmitted to the Gate; a boycott of the company leads to a fatwa, in which citizens are advised that "sin can be absolved by fasting, or by making seven consecutive phone calls, each one not separated by more than a month"
[Basma Abdel-Aziz – The Queue]

"All it took was for a lot of seemingly decent people to put the wrong person in power, and then pay for their innocent choice."
[Hugh Howey – Shift]

"We don't want to change. Every change is a menace to stability."
[Aldous Huxley – Brave New World]

A Virtue Of Disobedience

The main word for oppression in the Qur'ān comes from the trilateral verb z-l-m, of which there are many derivatives. The root according to the 'HdO Arabic-English Dictionary of Qur'ānic Usage, ' can mean:

> ...darkness, (of darkness) to descend; to put something in the wrong place, to act improperly; to cause someone to suffer a loss; to wrong someone, to act unjustly, injustice, tyranny, oppression.

From this trilateral root, there are fourteen derivative forms used, which occur on 315 occasions. Oppression is a concept that is frequently dealt with, and it is one that Muslims are forced to confront as a lived reality. The notion of oppression is not limited to a worldly understanding of rights being taken away from man, but also in terms of rights being taken away from Allāh, in other words disbelief. In that latter instance, another thing, person or entity is put in the place of Allāh's position, thereby us oppressing ourselves, as we have subverted the spiritual relationship.

The form of z-l-m that appears most frequently in the Qur'ān is zalim (pl. zaalimun), and this occurs as many as 126 times. This largely refers to those who have wronged themselves and others, and by virtue of that have become oppressors or committed an act of oppression.

I have wondered to myself, on many occasions, where does this oppression stem from? Why would human beings be so cruel to one another? When I meet trauma survivors who have escaped the barbarity of war or the cruelty of torture, it only ever reminds me of the need to end this form of oppression. However, that would mean understanding not only its source, but also its modalities. If I am correct about the cycles of trauma, then surely we should be able to think of oppression as form, rather than conception.

Iblis (the Devil) was commanded to prostrate to the first human creation of Allāh, the Prophet Adam, and he refused. This is the first chronological instance of Allāh describing an act of disobedience in the Qur'ān. Unlike the Christian tradition that sees the concept of original sin in the action of the Prophet Adam, it is Iblis who is described as being the one who disobeys a commandment of Allāh and who is thus rejected from grace.

The disobedience of Iblis is based on his arrogance, for he claims before Allāh that he cannot understand why it is that he, a being created from smokeless fire (jinn), is being commanded to bow before Adam, who is formed of clay. Before the soul of Adam was breathed into the mould, Iblis circled the clay and slipped inside it, fascinated and disturbed by how something so fragile, could be given a position of prominence in the heavens.

For me, Iblis projects the same racism that blights our contemporary world. His inability to see the best in Adam, to rather concentrate on form and not substance, results in his loss of grace before the sight of Allāh. This invocation of 'genetic' supremacy, is a reminder to all, that arrogance and jealousy that is derived from racist arguments, destroy the ability of one to see past the facade, and into the soul of another. We cannot even hope to begin to change the world, unless we see beyond what is superficial. Iblis, despite his knowledge of the heavens, despite his 'belief' in Allāh, despite his interaction with the angels, was not able to see past his own form, as simply another one of Allāh's creations.

Iblis goes...but not without a fight. He requests Allāh for a respite, at least until the End of Times in order to exact his revenge by leading human beings and jinn astray. Iblis's sole purpose, from the time of the creation of Adam until the end, is only to harm, in his unceasing desire for revenge.

I think about the Qurʾān, and how it describes the whisperings of 'shayatin', the lesser devils among human beings and jinn, who either knowingly or unknowingly play a role in this eternal spiritual conflict, one that takes the actions of this world, and places their consequences in both this life and the next.

As a psychologist, anthropologist and sociologist, Iblis has us beat. I'll have to be honest and say that I don't read his presence in the Qurʾān as a metaphor. My belief as a Muslim, is that he is real, and that he sees humans as his enemy. With that in mind, and believing that he and his jinn have the ability to 'whisper' in the hearts of men, I wonder about how much we are able to resist. After all, this being has been around for tens of thousands of years, and has had time to study the frailties of the human condition. In that regard, I want to think about his modalities of oppressing us, as the targets of his hate.

There is a prophetic tradition that relates the daily reporting practice of Iblis, when his minions return to provide a summary of their day's activities. They approach the throne of Iblis, one after another, explaining how they have been responsible for causing dissension on the Earth. In the narration, Iblis rejects each of these little devils, saying that they have done nothing of significance. That is until one comes to provide his report. He claims that he remained with a husband and wife non-stop until he was able to sow the seed of discord between them – it is this one that Iblis embraces and congratulates.

Divorce is permitted in Islam, and although frowned on by Allāh, carries with it a great deal of anxiety and hurt for those who have to experience its separation. To my mind, that is separate to the significance of the shayatin seeking the split, a modality of their oppression, rather than looking at the unfortunate result.

It is true that divorce is a terrible thing for anyone couple to endure. The Qur'ān dedicates large sections to the theory and practice of divorce even reminding Muslims to hold fast to the prayer, right in the middle of a long passage on the subject – as a reminder of what will assist them through such a difficult time. In many societies, divorce can often be like dropping a bomb in a crowd of people. Its impact is indiscriminate and devastating to the whole community. Often children are caught in its wake, in-laws, friendships, organisations and at many layers an emotional and physical detachment takes place.

My aim here is not to stigmatise divorce, as there are many good reasons why it may be necessary and can have life saving effects. However, I am more interested in why it is so precious to Iblis as a mode of action, specifically the act of splitting, and more so, why it pleases him.

It is the act of splitting apart, and its consequences that are so familiar as a tool of destruction in the world I see. If Iblis gives a sense of this modality of oppression in the spiritual world, then in the human world I turn my gaze towards Pharaoh, as the human manifestation of evil presented in the Qur'ān.

As I mentioned in the previous chapter, a third of the Qur'ān comprises of stories of the past, and the Prophetic story told more than any other, is that of Moses (Musa), the prophet of the Children of Israel. The struggle between Moses and Pharaoh, typifies the struggle between good and evil, the contest between righteousness and tyranny. The story is very familiar to those from the Judeo-Christian traditions especially in relation to the oppression of the Jews, the Children of Israel. The Qur'ān provides us an insight that I feel is almost central to the discussion of this chapter, and this is through a verse in the chapter Qassas:

> *Pharaoh made himself high and mighty in the land and divided people into different groups: one group he oppressed, slaughtering their sons and sparing their women – he was one of those who spread corruption.*[xviii]

I want to spend some time thinking about this verse. I come back to Timothy Snyder's recommendation of using history to instruct us, and I want to understand the points of instruction with which the oppression of Jews presents us. This verse from Qassas, in some ways is the whole story for me – for it speaks of the worst forms of oppression – the killing of children - universally accepted as the most innocent of all categories of human beings. How is it possible that Pharaoh was able to perpetuate such an evil against the Jews, an evil that was met without challenge? How can it be that we saw this same oppression take place again and again to the Jewish people? As Primo Levi described in the context of Auschwitz in 'If This is a Man':

> *This is the most immediate fruit of exile, of uprooting: the prevalence of the unreal over the real. Everyone dreamed past and future dreams, of slavery and redemption, of improbable paradises, of equally mythical and improbable enemies; cosmic enemies, perverse and subtle, who pervade everything like the air.*[xix]

The Children of Israel were not indigenously Egyptian. They lived in Egyptian society as an immigrant community facing exceptional difficulties throughout their time there. Long histories of the Children of Israel have been written in the Judaic tradition, but the Qur'ān here presents a layer of detail that is important for us to reflect upon. The verse quoted above makes mention of Pharaoh making himself high in the land and dividing his realm into different groups, after which he oppressed one group over others.

In this we see a predicate to the oppression of a single group: there must be a division of society along boundaries that will 'otherise' the specific group, whether that be along racial, class or religious lines. From the verse, it seems to me that it was only after the process of division, that Pharaoh began to kill the Children of Israel. Further, it should be noted that though it seems to be unsaid, all the other groups were not Jews. This made their division from the rest of the groups in society at the time even more stark and worth bearing in mind. There is of course, also the aspect that the other groups acquiesce the oppression of the Jews – we know little about how that took place, but it is worth thinking about – otherwise how would Pharaoh have made himself high and mighty in the land?

Michel Foucault helps us to understand this modality, albeit in the context of disciplining the individual:

> *But the principle of 'enclosure' is neither constant, nor indispensible, nor sufficient in disciplining machinery. This machinery works space in a much more flexible and detailed way. It does this first of all on the principle of elementary location or partitioning. Each individual has his own place; and each place its individual. Avoid distributions in groups; break up collective dispositions; analyse confused, massive or transient pluralities. Disciplinary space tends to be divided into as many sections as there are bodies or elements to be distributed. One must eliminate the effects of imprecise distributions, the uncontrolled disappearance of individuals, their diffuse circulation, their unusable and dangerous coagulation; it was a*

> *tactic of ant-desertion, anti-vagabondage, anti-concentration. Its aim was to establish presences and absences, to know where and how to locate individuals, to set up useful communication, to interrupt others, to be able at each moment to supervise the conduct of each individual, to assess it, to judge it, to calculate its qualities or merits. It was a procedure, therefore, aimed at knowing, mastering and using.[xx]*

Throughout history, there are numerous examples of how the divide-and-conquer tactic has been used as a precursor to total destruction. We know that much of the science of anthropology was born in genocide[xxi] – to meet the need of their empires to understand a people, and ultimately to destroy them.

Perhaps the most sophisticated version of this process was Operation Dalet, as described by the Israeli historian Ilan Pappe, which was carried out by the Zionists after years of mapping Palestinian villages and communities – the result was the Nakba (the Catastrophe) that would establish the state of Israel and displace hundreds of thousands Palestinians.[xxii] I think this is perhaps the most surprising of all cases, as the Jewish people are perfectly familiar with all the abuses that were perpetrated against them in the past, and yet somehow some of them who went on to be involved in political Zionism, perpetrated similar abuses against others.

But this type of intergenerational trauma - which underlines the notion developed in the previous chapter that time does not heal trauma, but rather can further it – brings with it its own complexities that need to be better understood. History is complicated, and the way it intersects with contemporary life is often difficult to discern, however, there were moments where others should have stepped up to assist the Jewish people.

During the late–1400s, King Ferdinand and Queen Isabella had forcefully converted the Jews of Spain to Christianity, known thereafter as the Conversos. The Conversos were systematically discriminated against based on their previous religious practices as recorded by Matthew Carr in his book 'Blood and Faith: The Purging of Muslim Spain'.[xxiii] However, up until the point of the forceful Jewish expulsion from Spain in 1492, what was the role played by Muslims in defending their Jewish counterparts? To what extent did they predict that the forceful conversions and discrimination being perpetrated against Jewish communities would come to haunt them over the next 120 years? I wonder how Allāh viewed any action they took, or indeed inaction, as something that was blameworthy in His eyes? Was this a Muslim moment of the bystander effect?

It is heartening to know that Sultan Bayezid II as ruler of the Ottomon Empire at the time, famously sent his naval Admiral Kemal Reis to help save the Jewish people from their fate of expulsion and provide them sanctuary.[xxiv] He famously called Ferdinand a fool for impoverishing the Spanish nation only to enrich his own lands.

In this, and throughout history, there are important lessons about witnessing oppression against others, and then standing by as a witness who does not act. I hope to examine this notion of witnessing oppression and what it means to be a witness in the next chapter.

In colonial India, the Muslims, and those from the Ulama (scholars) in particular, were deprecated. The British invested substantial effort in translating the classical Hanafi texts like Hidayah and Fataawa a-Hindiyya into English in a way that suited them. By codifying Islamic law into "Anglo-Muḥammadan" law the British were able to sever it from the Islamic juristic milieu. In doing so, it posited the British authority above all in matters relating the Sharia (corpus of Islamic practice) converting the substantive, dynamic and flexible fiqh (jurisprudence) into rigid, positive law.

Ironically, this did what reformist Muslims often accuse orthodox or traditional Islamic intellectuals of doing: closing the door of ijtihad (juristic exertion). Pertinently, it served the purpose of regulating and ultimately disposing aspects of Sharia. In the context of homicide, the governor Cornwallis complained that Islamic law was "founded on the most lenient principles and on an abhorrence of bloodshed".[xxv] In other words, Sharia was not 'barbaric' enough for the civilising British.

Unsurprisingly, this concern was tied to capitalist considerations. Nicolas Dirks observes that:

> *"British justice turned out to be far more draconian – in practice as well as in principle – than Islamic justice had been, resorting much more frequently to capital punishment... [The East India Company] was far more concerned with public order, and with the specific use of the law to protect its own trade and commerce as well as authority, than was the old regime"*[xxvi]

For the British in India, division was not just about formally splitting the society into atomised pieces (although they were masters of this tactic), but also redefining the boundaries of culture and religion in order to establish a sense of their own capitalist imperialist attitudes. The social engineering of cultural practices was crucial to the programme of repression.

The Pharaonic model, which I would say is the Iblis model of division before destruction, or divide and rule, is a narrative that has repeated itself over and again throughout history. It is also a story that is repeatedly told through fables and parables.

I want to think more carefully about the role that our own communities play in perpetuating harm against our own selves, but it is worth thinking about Apartheid as one of the example of how divide and rule worked to destabilise resistance.

Ever since I watched Denzel Washington's depiction of Bantu Steve Biko in the 1987 film 'Cry Freedom' as a child, I was horrified and obsessed with Apartheid – although I was young and could not understand the layers of oppression within the movie, I could clearly see and understand something horrible was taking place. Steve Biko is one of those voices that until this day moves me to action. Perhaps it was due to his young age when he began his activism, or the young age of 31 when his life was ended through a brutal attack by the Apartheid regime police in 1977. Biko was critical of the black tribal communities, who eventually collaborated with the Apartheid regime in order to establish their own fiefdoms within the structure of oppression:

> *Xhosas want their Transkei, the Zulus their Zululand etc. Coloured people harbour secret hopes of being classified as "brown Afrikaners" and therefore meriting admittance into the white laager while Indian people might be given a vote to swell the buffer zone between whites and Africans. Of course these promises will never be fulfilled---at least not in a hurry---and in the meantime the enemy bestrides South Africa like a colossus laughing aloud at the fragmented attempts by the powerless masses making appeals to his deaf ears.*
>
> *"The Transkei is the Achilles' heel of the*

Nationalists" claim intellectual politicians who are always quick to see a loophole even in a two-foot-thick iron wall. This is false logic. The Transkei, the CRC, Zululand and all these other apartheid institutions are modern-type laagers behind which the whites in this country are going to hide themselves for a long time to come. Slowly the ground is being swept off from under our feet and soon we as blacks will believe completely that our political rights are in fact in our "own" areas. Thereafter we shall find that we have no leg to stand on in making demands for any rights in "mainland White South Africa" which incidentally will comprise more than three-quarters of the land of our forefathers.[xxvii]

Biko's description reminds me of a story in the Arab world, a story that is told of three bulls who are approached by a lion that desires to eat them. The lion is aware that on his own he cannot take these three bulls while they are together, but notices that they are coloured differently, one is black, one is white, and one is red. The lion devises a strategy that will allow him to eat at least one of them, and so he approaches the red and white bull, saying that the black bull is different from them, and that if they permit him to eat the black bull, he will leave them alone. On conferring, the red and white bull acquiesce, saying that they will still be strong enough to take on the lion, should they need to, and this way the lion will be fed and leave them alone. The lion has his fill, however, this is a situation that does not last. Our lion is hungry again. So this time he approaches the white bull, and explains that actually, while the black bull was tasty, he wasn't large enough to satiate his need, and so if he were also to eat the red bull, there would be no need to approach the white bull at all. On consideration (or lack thereof) the white bull acquiesces to this, and so the lion ate the red bull too. After a while, as the white bull sees the lion's steady approach, he sees everything clearly from the moment he was first approached. With a regretful sigh, he cries to the lion, "You killed me, the day you killed the black bull."

That is the thing about oppression. When we divide ourselves to allow a law that treats one portion of society unequally, those laws will still be in effect after that group is gone. Those laws will still be required; as such oppressive systems require fuel to keep their fires going. Without an enemy, without an outsider to feed those flames, those in power will lose their position of control.

When moving between historic and contemporary understanding of oppression, repression and violence, it's important to highlight that the method of repression today is historically unprecedented, thanks to a state which has made integral to its inception and its subsistence both structural and overt violence.

In other words, efficiency is unparalleled, thanks to the number of police, the militarisation of the police, and of course the unique feature of the modern state – the technological tour de force that is the surveillance apparatus. Systemic surveillance brings about a more effective oppression machine. Thus, all forms of modern warfare ultimately become tools of terror, as described by Gregoire Chamayou:

> *In making combat impossible and transforming armed combat into execution, the aim is to annihilate the very willpower of those opposing them. As Charles Dunlap, a major general in the U.S. Air Force, explains, "Death per se does not extinguish the will to fight in such opponents; rather, it is the hopelessness that*

arises from the inevitability of death from a source they cannot fight." He goes on to say, "The precision and persistence of today's airpower creates opportunities to dislocate the psychology of the insurgents." The idea is not a new one. In the twentieth century, Sir John Bagot Glubb had already expressed it in very similar terms when speaking of the aerial bombing by means of which the British put down native rebellions in the interwar period: "Their tremendous moral effect is largely due to the demoralization engendered in the tribesman by his feeling of helplessness and his inability to reply effectively to the attack."[xxviii]

There are times, when the response to oppression can be oppressive itself, when it can go beyond not only what the law allows, but what the ethics of decency and morality permit. Not decency and morality as established by coloniser/occupier/oppressor, but from what is intrinsic to our own traditions – as the celebrated Libyan resistance fighter Omar al-Mukhtar once famously said, "They are not our teachers." For me, this has given rise to key questions of our time. How do we understand non-state violence, in a world filled with state-sanctioned violence? How do we perceive these non-state actors, and to what extent can we understand or condemn them for the actions they have taken? These are pressing issues, and ones we need to confront. How do we differentiate between those engaged in political violence and the state that engages in its own versions of political violence – how do we try and bring understanding into these cycles of violence and so end them?

Let me turn back to our example of the converted Muslims living in Spain (Moriscos) during the 1500s. Between 1511 to 1526, Ferdinand and Isabella had heightened the activities of the Spanish Inquisition, leading to a multitude of abuses against the Morisco people. 'Old Christian' priests would often take advantage of the authority they had been given and climb into the rooms of young Morisca women to rape them. Due to the impunity these priests had, there was nothing the town could do to ward off the advances and often people simply had to accept the situation. The continued general environment resulted in Farex Aben Farex leading a group of 100 Morisco men to carry out a massacre in the Alpujarras on Christmas Eve in 1568 where the clergy class where targeted and killed for their abuse.[xxix] Writing of this incident, the Christian chronicler Diego Hurtado de Mendoza wrote:

> *These crimes were committed partly by people whom we had persecuted for vengeance, partly by the monfíes whose way of life had so conditioned them to cruelty that cruelty had become part of their natures.*[xxx]

European history is littered with examples of how when repression is the tactic of power asserting itself, it often results in new forms of violence that are further repressed. This is the cycle of violence and trauma that as a theme, recurs throughout this book. In the post-French Revolution period, the European monarchies were fearful of the ideology of the Enlightenment, and sought to repress it as best they could – resulting in a Europe-wide security apparatus resplendent with informants, spies, security agencies and abuses. During the period, the British Minister to Florence, Lord Burghersh expressed caution of these responses, and predicted how the actions of the state would not lead to increased security:

> *I am neither a Radical, nor that I have so far forgotten the principles which I have been brought up in, not to view with disgust the*

> *spirit of subversion and Jacobinism which is*
> *abroad; but I must at the same time declare that*
> *the system pursued by the Austrians in Italy, the*
> *ungenerous treatment of the Italians subjected*
> *to their government, will, as long as it is*
> *persisted in ... not add one jot to their*
> *security!*[xxxi]

What such contexts give us, is an instruction from history, that repression and exceptional security measures do not lead to a reduction in violence - quite the opposite in fact - they could lead to increases in violence. The US-led global War on Terror has been raging across the world since 12 September 2001, and in that time, international peace and stability has not increased one bit. Rather, all the countries that were invaded by the US and her allies are worse off than they were before, and new fronts of political violence have opened up where previously there were none.

Scholars such as the former CIA psychiatrist Marc Sageman question the entire basis on which Muslims are considered to be a threat, and so advocates a strong pull back on the measures that have been installed in western secular democracies:

> *However, the new trend in political violence*
> *has halted this march to liberalism, and Western*
> *states have partially rolled back some of these*
> *freedoms. In Britain, freedom of expression has*
> *been limited to prevent the "glorification of*
> *terrorism." In France, laws against*
> *"participation in an association of malefactors*
> *whose goals is to prepare a terrorist act" erode*
> *freedom of association. In the United States,*
> *where freedom of speech and association are*
> *enshrined in the First Amendment of the*
> *Constitution, the government prosecutes*
> *suspected terrorists using laws against vaguely*

> *defined crimes such as conspiracies and material support for terrorism. The scope of these laws has been dramatically expanded over the past two decades and allows entrapment of naive Muslim militants into committing crimes that would never have occurred absent FBI inducement. As a result, most Western liberal democracies have watered down individual civil rights and locked up people they label terrorists in what amounts to preventive detention.[xxxii]*

Living as a Muslim within my own suspect community in the UK, the presentation of my own brothers and sisters as a threat is out of congruence with what I know about them. We all attend mosques and know our communities well enough to know that we have far greater problems than our young being attracted by political violence - this is not their primary concern at all. As Sageman expresses so well, the response to the potential threat is not only overkill, but will eventually make matters worse.

There is of course, an elephant in the room; the fact that Muslims have been involved in political violence. How do I, as a Muslim, understand my response to this? I can claim as much as I like that the terrorist threat is minimal compared to other types of harm, but then one person could take multiple lives through a simple and unsophisticated act of violence. It is not just me, this is a voice I hear in our communities, and those outside of our communities, as the fear sets in. Should this fear confuse us though? Should it permit us to change our values, our way of life, our protections? Is the response of the last sixteen years justified by the threat? I do not think so. I'm reminded of the Bene Gesserit litany in Frank Herbert's 'Dune':

> *I must not fear. Fear is the mind-killer. Fear is*

> *the little-death that brings total obliteration. I*
> *will face my fear. I will permit it to pass over me*
> *and through me. And when it has gone past I*
> *will turn the inner eye to see its path. Where the*
> *fear has gone there will be nothing. Only I will*
> *remain.*

Fear is the little death that brings total obliteration - a fitting description for worldwide counterterrorism policy post 9/11. I am inclined towards another route entirely. I do not want people to fear Muslims. I do not want Muslims to fear overreaching repercussions. I do not want my country, the UK, to sacrifice its own notions of justice, chasing phantoms that might never emerge, and even if they do emerge, to not lose ourselves in the response. What I am sure of, is that more understanding is needed so everything that can be placed in its correct context and responses can be effective.

Returning to Biko, his incisiveness in thinking of the lives of black people in South Africa and what they needed remains as relevant today as it was then. He understood, that at the centre of the fears that black people had, was the structural violence of the state (a notion I will return to later):

> *It is this fear that erodes the soul of black people*
> *in South Africa--- a fear obviously built up*
> *deliberately by the system through a myriad of*
> *civil agents, be they post office attendants,*
> *police, CID officials, army men in uniform,*
> *security police or even the occasional trigger-*
> *happy white farmer or store owner. It is a fear*
> *so basic in the considered actions of black people*
> *as to make it impossible for them to behave like*
> *people---let alone free people. From the attitude*
> *of a servant to his employer, to that of a black*
> *man being served by a white attendant at a*

shop, one sees this fear clearly showing through. How can people be prepared to put up a resistance against their overall oppression if in their individual situations, they cannot insist on the observance of their manhood? This is a question that often occurs to overseas visitors who are perceptive enough to realise that all is not well in the land of sunshine and milk.

Yet this is a dangerous type of fear, for it only goes skin deep. It hides underneath it an immeasurable rage that often threatens to erupt. Beneath it lies naked hatred for a group that deserves absolutely no respect. Unlike in the rest of the French or Spanish former colonies where chances of assimilation made it not impossible for blacks to aspire towards being white, in South Africa whiteness has always been associated with police brutality and intimidation, early morning pass raids, general harassment in and out of townships and hence no black really aspires to being white. The claim by whites of monopoly on comfort and security has always been so exclusive that blacks see whites as the major obstacle in their progress towards peace, prosperity and a sane society. Through its association with all these negative aspects, whiteness has thus been soiled beyond recognition. At best therefore blacks see whiteness as a concept that warrants being despised, hated, destroyed and replaced by an aspiration with more human content in it.[xxxiii]

How can we begin to find this 'human content'? I believe this question is central to reframing our entire discourse of securitisation and fear.

For the last decade, I have been fortunate enough to work with legal teams in the US as a consultant on their mitigation cases. Under the 18 U.S. Code §3592, a provision is made that both mitigating and aggravating factors can be considered when making a determination on whether or not the death penalty can be applied to seriously violent crimes. Having been involved in exclusively building mitigation cases, I have learnt that when you take a multi-generational social history of a client, there will almost always be circumstances behind why that individual committed a violent crime. These circumstances are important to bear in mind. That does not necessitate that the person should be released from custody, but it does mean that a degree of understanding must be exercised by the court in order to be fair to the individual, and not seek violent retribution against him/her.

As a Muslim coming to the US concept of mitigation, I was immediately enamoured with it. I found there to be so much mercy and justice in this one idea as it conveyed so much of the practice of Islam's first judge, the Prophet Muḥammad. He would earnestly mitigate the punishment of the Qur'ānic offences himself, seeking an excuse to try and give those who he was to judge a way out – a practice that was found later again with his successors and most famously with the second Caliph of Islam, Umar ibn al-Khattab. I found this same sentiment being brought in the US justice system through mitigation, with the difference that it is the defence that has to prove the mitigation case, while the prosecution attempts to undermine it - the judge plays little role except to weigh the evidence.

What about the violence of non-state actors? Is there perhaps something that we could learn from this practice of mitigation that might allow us the space not to fall into fear? There is a verse in the Qur'ān that I have started to refer to as the verse of mitigation, and it appears in the chapter al-Baqarah. The context of this verse is that the Prophet Muḥammad sent a group of men under the command of 'Abdullah ibn Jahsh with instructions to reach a place known as Nakhlah. When they completed their task, they began to make their way to their home city of Madinah when they came across a man from the enemy Quraysh who they killed. The men were unaware they had killed someone during the forbidden months, and so a great complaint was raised by the Quraysh – much to the consternation of the Prophet himself who did not approve of this action. The Muslims were insulted for breaking this ancient Arab custom – a custom that the Prophet approved and respected. It was in response to this incident though, that Allāh corrected the Prophet and provided some mitigation to the offence:

> They ask you [Prophet] about fighting in the sacred month. Say, 'Fighting in that month is a great offence, but to bar others from God's path, to disbelieve in Him, prevent access to the Sacred Mosque, and expel its people, are still greater offences in God's eyes: persecution is worse than killing. [xxxiv]

In the eyes of Allāh, the persecution by the Quraysh against all those who had come up against them and their disbelief, was far greater a sin than this individual killing. Allāh does not whitewash the offence, He calls it out for what it is, but places the offence within a much larger context. This, right here, is the standard by which Muslims should judge all actions – not allowing their fear to take control, but seeing everything in the cold light of the day. I want to see responses to be based around facts and context. I am reminded of the pressure that was brought to bear on Martin Luther King Jr, when he took a position against the war Vietnam and considered the question of violence:

> As I have walked among the desperate, rejected, and angry young men, I have told them that

Molotov cocktails and rifles would not solve their problems. I have tried to offer them my deepest compassion while maintaining my conviction that social change comes most meaningfully through nonviolent action. But they asked, and rightly so, "What about Vietnam?" They asked if our own nation wasn't using massive doses of violence to solve its problems, to bring about the changes it wanted. Their questions hit home, and I knew that I could never again raise my voice against the violence of the oppressed in the ghettos without having first spoken clearly to the greatest purveyor of violence in the world today: my own government.[xxxv]

I want to see leadership in that regard, not fallacious statements that are made out of fear or out of the creation of false expectations that further undermine our communities. We should judge each and every action by those who commit violence, within the totality of their contexts, from mental health, abuse, to wider political circumstances - then, and only then can we lay claim to having 'understood'. In that sense, Edward W Said has provided us with important markers by which to understand our 'now', to be able to fully assess the extent of where we are:

We allow justly that the Holocaust has permanently altered the consciousness of our time: why do we not accord the same epistemological mutation in what imperialism has done, and what Orientalism continues to do? Think of the line that starts with Napoleon, continues with the rise of Oriental studies and the takeover of North Africa, and goes on in similar undertakings in Vietnam, in Egypt, in Palestine and, during the entire twentieth

> *century, in the struggle over oil and strategic*
> *control in the Gulf, in Iraq, Syria, Palestine and*
> *Afghanistan. Then think contrapuntally of the*
> *rise of anti-colonial nationalism, through the*
> *short period of liberal independence, the era of*
> *military coups, of insurgency, civil war,*
> *religious fanaticism, irrational struggle and*
> *uncompromising brutality against the latest*
> *bunch of "natives." Each of these phases and eras*
> *produces its own distorted knowledge of the*
> *other, each its own reductive images, its own*
> *disputatious polemics.*[xxxvi]

We cannot separate the world we see, and the violence we see in particular from the actions, narratives and the epistemologies that have shaped the world around us. To understand the resultants from the war in Iraq, one must understand ALL of the elements that went into the production of the actors operating there, such as the Islamic State, from their specific circles of history.

What of the criminal though? Should he be left alone because of a wider circumstance that made his life difficult? Here the Prophet Muḥammad provides the answer: help your brother whether he is oppressed or the oppressor. When the Prophet's companions heard this, they did not understand what he meant and sought clarification, how can one help the oppressor? The Prophet replied, by stopping his oppression. It is a remarkably simple statement, but one that is full of meaning for me. The Prophet did not excommunicate the oppressor, but rather called him a brother, one that needed to be stopped. I will be honest: I do not know if I have that degree of love and patience in my heart that the Prophet is expecting of us here. It is a high and noble standard to see someone who is involved in oppression, and still consider them to be your brother.

How does one achieve that? I wish I knew the answer, for I meet survivors of oppressive practices all the time, and my rage is nearly always directed at those who harmed them.

It is difficult to achieve anything alone (although not impossible) and as I circle back in my mind to the start of this chapter, I see a large and long self-perpetuating conflict before me, but also the micro-aggressions that take place on a daily basis – these are all manifestations of oppression. The one modality that seems to be consistent across everything I described, however, is this idea of division, or disunity. If this is what Iblis wants, if this is how Pharaoh operated, if this is how every oppressive tyrant, dictator and despot sought to control and harm their populations, then surely the panacea to such a trend is to reverse it? This is not some grand plan. Rather it is a simple principle. A principle that was recognised by Martin Luther King Jr in one of the later speeches of his life, using Pharaoh's tactic of division to make his point:

> *You know, whenever Pharaoh wanted to prolong the period of slavery in Egypt, he had a favorite formula for doing it. What was that? He kept the slaves fighting among themselves. But whenever the slaves get together, something happens in Pharaoh's court, and he cannot hold the slaves in slavery. When the slaves get together, that' the beginning of getting out of slavery. Now let us maintain unity.*[xxxvii]

Unity takes real effort though. It requires many actions of the heart to see past the smaller things that divide us, particularly when before us looms an edifice of oppression. I ask myself and I ask you as well, if your house is on fire, do you stop to rearrange the pictures that have gone askew? If the house was not on fire, the pictures would seem like a big deal – the slant they are on would be considered to be wholly unacceptable and you would wish to straighten it...but during a fire...drop all else! Put out the fire, there is time to straighten the pictures (read 'ourselves') later. We can even argue about where to put the furniture.

Now, more than ever, we need one another. We need to unite, not just among ourselves as Muslim groups, but in our private lives, within our organisations, with those who will stand by us both inside and outside of our traditions. Only then, can we really have a chance at bringing about systemic change, not just the superficial variety where we remove one class of oppressor to replace him/her with another. Let this be part of our modality of resistance.

A Community of Witnesses

A Virtue Of Disobedience

"Back to Germany," one of the cops said, surveying him. "I'm an American," Frank Frink said. "You're a Jew," the cop said."
[Philip K Dick – The Man in the High Castle]

"The woman's got one hand on his chest and every time she tips forward she's giving him a crackle across his torso. He's trying to push her hand away, and screaming, and reaching out to the crowd around them for help, and begging in a slurred language Roxy wouldn't understand, except that the sound of 'Help me, oh God, help me' is the same in every language."
[Naomi Alderman – The Power]

"A country that tolerates evil means- evil manners, standards of ethics- for a generation, will be so poisoned that it never will have any good end."
[Sinclair Lewis – It's Can't Happen Here]

I am a witness.

It is this one truth that constantly displaces my comforts and privileges. I walk around London and see all those who are living in extreme poverty. I see my fellow countrymen resorting to food banks in order to have the basic dignity of having food in their stomachs. I see the structural racism that is perpetrated against black people, denying them so much in every part of their lives...I see so much injustice with my own eyes.

The media then widens my lens.

No longer is my witnessing of oppression limited to bypassing a homeless person on the street, my view of oppression in the world is expanded to Guantanamo Bay, to the plight of the Uighur in China, to the Rohingya in Myanmar and so on.

And then social media widens my lens further.

Now I witness bombs dropping on the heads of Syrian children. I am a witness to the executions of Muslims and non-Muslims by violent groups with the claim that it is some form retaliation in the name of religion. I can immediately understand the plight of Palestinian children living in the world's largest open-air prison in Gaza.

And by the act of witnessing them, they have obligations on me.

What does it mean to be a witness living in the world today? In many ways there are far too many issues for a single person to take on, to try and fight back against. I remind myself of the Prophet Muḥammad's advice, that if as a Muslim I witness a wrong, then I should change it with my hand, and if I cannot, then to change it with my tongue, and if I cannot do that, then to at least to change it with my heart. There is a baseline of behaviour I know I can fulfil: I can at the very least speak to my heart to find sympathy and empathy for all those who have been wronged, while directing my indignation towards those who oppress.

..the crowd gathered round the scaffold, it was not simply to witness the sufferings of the condemned man or to excite the anger of the executioner: it was also to hear an individual who had nothing more to lose curse the judges, the laws, the government and religion. The public execution allowed the luxury of these momentary saturnalia, when nothing remained to prohibit or to punish. Under the protection of imminent death, the criminal could say everything and the crowd cheered. If there were annals in which the last words of the tortured and executed were scrupulously recorded, and if one had the courage to read through them, even if one did no more than question the vile populace that gathers around the scaffolds out of cruel curiosity, one would be told that no one who had died on the wheel did not accuse heaven for the misery that brought him to the crime, reproach his judges for their barbarity, curse the minister of the altars who accompanies them...[xxxviii]

The quote from Michel Foucault speaks to me about the spectacle of injustice, and the proximity of the witnesses to those injustices. Those watching an execution take place, are not only there in order to be a witness to the spectacle, but also witnesses to the environment that the spectacle permits. For Foucault, they are there not just out of cruel fascination of the act of killing, but to bear witness to words that will be spoken truthfully in an environment where the truth cannot be spoken, albeit fleetingly.

According to the 'HdO Dictionary of Qur'ānic Usage' the Arabic trilateral root sh-h-d appears 158 times in thirteen different forms with the meaning:

...landmark; presence, to witness, to testify to

what one has witnessed, seen or beheld with one's own eyes; to be or become a martyr.

Lina Mounzer's tragically beautiful essay 'War in Translation', takes the explanation of this root further:

> *In Arabic, the root of the verb, to witness, is sh-h-d. Roots are important in Arabic. They are present, that is, known and recognizable, not obscure etymologies but immediate and close, giving life directly to all the words that bud and branch from them. From the three-letter root verb, you make the subject and the object, but also adjectives, adverbs and a whole host of other, more complex verbs, subjects and objects related to the first. Even these words—subject, verb, object—are more directly related in Arabic. Translated literally, the subject is the doer, the verb is the doing, the object the one it is done to. In English, a writer writes a book; a letter. In Arabic, al-katib yaktubu kitab; maktoob. All from the root k-t-b, to write. From "to witness," we get shahed, the one who witnesses; mashhad, the spectacle or the scene, but also shaheed, martyr; istishhad, to be martyred, to die for a cause. As if the act of bearing witness, followed to the end of one of its branches, snaps under the weight of what is seen, and you fall to your death. As if to die for a cause in Arabic is to bear witness to something until it annihilates the self.[xxxix]*

It would seem that the process of witnessing, in life and death, has significance over the course of entire human interaction. I am a witness in my faith, as much as I am a witness to the world around me. The primacy of these can be found in a verse in the chapter al-'Anaam in the Qur'ān, where Allāh says:

> *Say, "What thing is greatest in testimony?" Say,*

*"Allāh is witness between me and you. And this
Qur'ān was revealed to me that I may warn you
thereby and whomever it reaches. Do you [truly]
testify that with Allāh there are other deities?"
Say, "I will not testify [with you]." Say, "Indeed,
He is but one God, and indeed, I am free of
what you associate [with Him]."*[xl]

In the world of Muslims, the testification or
witnessing to Monotheism or the single unity of Allāh
is associated with the first act of becoming a Muslim.
There is no Islam for a human being who does not
witness the phrase that enters them into the
community of Islam: I bear witness that there is no god
except Allāh, and I bear witness that Muḥammad is His
messenger. This witnessing is done both with the heart,
so that the heart accepts that this is the case, but it also
done with the tongue, so that it becomes actualised.

I want to interrogate this witnessing further. What are
the extents of it? How can we understand its
significance to the world around us and also to the
history of the world as Muslims know it? Following on
from the theme of using history as a tool of instruction,
I am reminded of the story of Khabab ibn Arrat. He
was reminiscing of the time of torture during the
period of persecution after the death of the Prophet
Muḥammad. Those looking on the marks of torture on
Khabab's back remarked that they had never seen
anything like it, and so he explained that hot stones
would be placed on his back by his persecutors, until
he could smell his own fat burning. When Khabab
asked the Prophet to pray to God to alleviate their
suffering, he was told:

*[In times] before you, a [believing] man would
be seized and [a pit] would be dug for him in the
ground, into which he would be placed. A saw
would then be brought and placed on his head,*

[and his head would be sawed] until it split into two halves. His flesh would be combed with iron combs until it was removed from his bones. But that did not distance him from his religion...By Allāh, Allāh will complete this affair [and grant victory to the religion] such that a rider will travel from San'ā' to Hadhramawt, fearing none other than Allāh - and the wolf over his sheep - but you are impatient."[xli]

The Prophet had become upset with Khabab for being dispirited and feeling inferior, as relatively things had not been as difficult for those in the past – he was trying to motivate Khabab. It seems there is a theme that is consistent in the Qur'ān which relates to those who in extraordinary circumstances bear witness to the unity of Allāh, and who are tested with their beliefs. Then we are told how they respond to those threats by remaining true. I have found no departure in the entirety of the Qur'ān to this position, but it is important to still understand this process further.

Before I begin to delve more deeply into the story of the People/Companions of the Ditch, I wanted to acknowledge that this thinking was very much developed through discussions with Dr Uthmaan Lateef, who posited this theory of witnessing to me in the first place. Without reproducing the entirety of the story, it is important to know that there were a people in an unknown period in the past, who believed in Allāh after a witnessing a contest between a boy and an oppressive King – where the King's killing of the boy resulted in them accepting Allāh as their only God. The final part of the Prophetic narration relates what happens next:

The King was then told, "Do you see what you feared? By Allāh, that which you feared has happened! The people have believed [in the

> *Lord of the boy]." So [the King] ordered for*
> *ditches [to be dug] at the junctions of all the*
> *roads. When they were dug, fires were lit in*
> *them and [the King] said, "Whoever does not*
> *renounce his religion, then throw him in [the*
> *fire], or tell them to jump into it." So this was*
> *what happened, until a woman came carrying a*
> *baby, and she hesitated to jump into the fire, so*
> *her child said to her, "O Mother! Have patience,*
> *for you are upon the Truth!"[xlii]*

Although different in its story and presentation of the key facts, there is a story within the Christian tradition that bears some stark similarities to the story as it is told by the Prophet Muḥammad, and also in the Qur'ān. Simeon of Beth Arsham describes the sixth century incident of a community of Christians who are massacred by Jews at the Syriac town of Najran (the Islamic version locates the same town).[xliii] There is the similarity of requirements by an unjust king for the believers to revoke their faith, the building of a large fire, the mass execution of the believers, and significantly, the desire of a woman to be burnt alive by joining those already being burnt, rather than to renounce faith:

> *The Jews amassed all the martyrs' bones and*
> *brought them into the church, where they*
> *heaped them up. They then brought in the*
> *priests, deacons, subdeacons, readers, and "sons*
> *and daughters of the covenant," and laymen*
> *and women as well. . . . They filled the church*
> *up from wall to wall, some 2000 persons*
> *according to the men who came from Najran;*
> *then they piled up wood all round the outside of*
> *the church and set alight to it, thus burning the*
> *church along with everyone inside it.[xliv]*

The story of the boy and the king is not explicated in

the Qur'ān, but it does speak about it in the chapter al-Buruj, in particular making reference to the torture and sacrifice of the people who believed:

> *By the sky with its towering constellations, by the promised Day, by witness and witnessed, perish the makers of the trench, of fuel-stoked fire! They sat down and witnessed what they were doing to the believers. Their only grievance against them was their faith in God, the Mighty, the Praiseworthy, to whom all control over the heavens and earth belongs: God is witness over all things.*[xlv]

Allāh describes in these verses a number of witnesses. There are those who are witnesses to the torture and mass executions themselves, then there are the heavens who witness this event, and significantly, Allāh describes Himself as being a witness to these events. This ditch that was dug, and the fire that was stoked in order to carry out this mass killing, was something that was seen, related and condemned. Allāh explains that there was no case against the killing of these people, except that they believed in Him alone and refused to obey the king – but perhaps what is more shocking, is the language that is used to describe the method of killing. When Allāh describes that killers, 'sat down', He does not use the more commonly used word 'julus', meaning to just sit, He uses the Arabic word 'qu'ud' meaning to sit in a leisurely way, but can also mean in the 'HdO Dictionary of Quranic Usage', to deny help to others. These killers were not just witnessing the impact of their evil acts, but went further in enjoying the sight before them. They relished in their killing.

Regardless of belief in the stories that the Qur'ān presents as being accurate, one does not need to go so far back in history to understand this point. The Holocaust is perhaps one of the most disgraceful reminders of how individuals can be involved in mass executions, but also how they can enjoy the spectacle before them. On reading Laurence Rees's 'The Holocaust', I was immediately reminded of the People of the Ditch when I read of the sitting of the Nazis at the Auschwitz-Birkenau concentration camp:

> *He tried to understand how the SS could be responsible for the appalling cruelty in front of them, and yet still consider themselves civilised. In Birkenau he had heard the camp's orchestra playing pieces by German, Austrian and Italian composers. SS men were sitting by the crematorium where children, mothers, women and men were burning but they were just sitting there. Now I think that they were just pleased to have properly completed their work and were due for a cultural entertainment – they had no dilemmas. The wind from the Birkenau blew the smell from the death camp in but they were just sitting and listening to Mozart and others, this is what a being is capable of.*[xlvi]

The targeting of a group based on belief, the fire, the women and children, the leisurely sitting – it is all there – as if it were a verbatim description of what happened to the People of the Ditch. I believe in the Qur'ān, and have faith that everything described is a matter of fact – and yet there remains somewhat of a disconnect to stories such as the People of the Ditch. In the modern context, ditches of Jewish bodies, of Bosnian bodies, of Rohingya bodies make these verses come alive, for here we have empirical proof that human beings – if human is still an appropriate descriptor – are capable of the worst excesses of violence against one another. We have been and are witnesses to these excesses.

In that sense, I am always nauseated by the language

that is used by others to describe people of other faiths and traditions. I refuse to subscribe to name-calling or using blunt stereotypes to describe others – it can only ever lead to dehumanisation. For that reason, I have always loved the verse in the Qur'ān in the chapter al-Hujarat:

> *People, We created you all from a single man and a single woman, and made you into races and tribes so that you should get to know one another. In God's eyes, the most honoured of you are the ones most mindful of Him: God is all knowing, all aware.*[xlvii]

This verse levels the playing field of races, and rather establishes a hierarchy based on righteousness, of being mindful towards Allāh – a notion that I wish to return to soon. I find this verse compelling especially due to some of the dehumanising language that is used by my own co-religionists against others. I am thinking here in particular of the disgraceful references that are used in the Arabic-speaking world to black people as 'abeed' or slave. Those who are called out, say it is meaningless and they do not mean any harm by it, but its roots and implications are entirely racist.

Even within my own Pakistani culture, you will often hear of elders describing prospective girls for marriage as ideally being 'gori chitti' or in other words, perfectly white. They have internalised standards of beauty even among their own people that have nothing to do with how 'good' a person might be – rather they focus on the superficial as a false standard by which to judge the 'goodness' of others. In India, Unilever has been marketing their 'Fair & Lovely' skin-whitening product since 1975, holding now somewhere between 50-70% of the $200 million skin-whitening market.[xlviii] According to Unilever subsidiary company, Hindustan Lever Limited (HLL), the use of skin-whitening cream is:

> *"aspirational.... A fair skin is like education, regarded as a social and economic step up"*[xlix]

This internalised racism turns inwards, so that it establishes resentment of the self, drawing lines of demarcation over the superficial to meet the coloniser's expectations of what is considered to be acceptable. In her autobiography, Assata Shakur describes that as a child, they would use the word black as being synonymous with being ugly, black bodies became a site of self-harm:

> *But behind our fights, self-hatred was clearly visible.*
>
> *"Nappy head, nappy head, I catch your ass, you goin' be dead."*
>
> *"You think you Black and ugly now; I'm gonna beat you till you purple."*
>
> *"You just another nigga to me. Ima show you what I do with niggas like you."*
>
> *"You better shut your big blubber lips."*
>
> *We would call each other "jungle bunnies" and "bush boogies". We would talk about each other's ugly, big lips and flat noses. We would call each other pickaninnies and nappy-haired so-and-so's,*[l]

What do we do when confronted with such gross references? Are we guilty of the bystander effect when dehumanised language is given oxygen and we do not speak out against others, and even ourselves? In this regard, I want to think about some verses in the Qur'ān that relate to a story known as the People of Saturday or the Sabbath (Ashab al-Sabt). This was a community of Jews living in the past who were commanded by Allāh not to work on the Sabbath. A group from among this Jewish community would throw out their nets on a Friday, and retrieve them on a Sunday, claiming that actually they had done nothing wrong by doing so. Another group amongst this community spoke out against them, and the last group remained silent – claiming that they did not want to interfere in the business of others.

Allāh's treatment of the different groups is telling in relation to the concept of witnessing. As for the group who breached the order, Allāh describes that He condemned them in their life by turning them into monkeys and pigs, and them condemned them in the afterlife as well. As for the ones who spoke out, they were promised paradise, while the group who remained silent, some of the scholars say that Allāh remained silent about their fate until the Day of Judgment. For those who use the monkeys and pigs reference as a point of disparaging Jews, then perhaps they forget that a group of believers among them were promised with paradise. They had witnessed the wrongdoing and spoke out against it.

In relation to the concept of witnessing, I am also intrigued by the group who remained silent, and Allāh's silence about their fate. Being a witness it seems is not enough – not without some kind of act connected to it. If you witness, and do not act, does that leave you condemned?

Here I return to my original question: how can I be a witness to so much injustice, and feel comfortable with the world around me? This is the hardest of all questions to answer, as the claims on time are so competing. Over the last three months, I have witnessed acts of violence being carried out against my neighbours and fellow countrymen in the UK by those who claim to share the same faith as me – I don't recognise the targeting of civilians at pop concerts as being from anything that mildly represents the tradition of resisting oppression or fighting against injustice – for me this is nihilism. This type of act should not be confused – as there is a concept of fighting for self-determination, against alien occupation and apartheid-style racism – and yet the noble is always conflated with the ignoble.

I share something with those I live with. I share their sense of humour, popular culture references, cultural cues that for those outside of the UK setting would be lost completely – and so we recognise one another and share something profound due to our proximity. The UK is my home, and I am British – there are no two ways about it. The verse in al-Hujarat suggests that we learn to recognise people from other races and other traditions, but I don't need to learn to recognise the British, for I am one of them.

This is where for some it becomes tricky. If you ask some Muslims, they will tell you sternly that there is no possibility of being British and Muslim – as if they are mutually exclusive – I disagree. Saying this, I want to better understand the multiple identities that I have, and how they interact with one another. This is complicated enough by race, without throwing a religion with a very strong sense of its own identity in to the mix.

Reni Eddo-Lodge attempts to ask some very difficult questions in her excellent book 'Why I'm No Longer Talking to White People About Race'. In an interview she conducts with a mixed-race British national, Jessica explains how her black identity emerged as she began to reflect on the attitudes that she encountered even within her own family:

> *my uncle and my cousin have been quite...well, they've been really racist. Sharing things on Facebook, sharing Britain First stuff, sharing stuff about "ban the burqa". I've been trying to*

have conversations with them about why that's racist and that's hurtful to me as well, and [I'm] just not getting anywhere. They see me talking about race as if I'm the problem, as if I'm the troublemaker. It's caused me to distance myself over the last couple of years from my white family.[li]

Identity formation is complicated. My ethnically Pakistani, culturally half-English half-Welsh children display all sorts of wonderful combinations of identity that I find interesting to observe. They pronounce the word 'tooth' as 'tuth' as a Welshism, just one of many examples (they get that from their mother), despite living and being educated in England. They support Cardiff FC due to their Welsh cousins, but more interestingly, support Wales over England in the Rugby (or anything). Fortunately Wales don't have a specific cricket team of their own, so they don't have worry about multiple layers of the Tebbit test!

As communities, we tend to focus on our own first, and a form of tribalism emerges where we find a sense of solidarity with those closest to our culture, values and ideals. This is perhaps exemplified in the western world from the culture of solidarity that has emerged out of acts of terrorism or political violence. Whether in France, UK, Belgium, Germany or wherever they took place, large gatherings of world leaders, the lighting of monuments represent a sense of solidarity that the European nations, in particular, feel for one another. Again, Reni Eddo-Lodge highlights this culture after the November 2015 Paris attacks, but juxtaposed to another significant attack in Kenya that had done place seven months previously:

Here, it seemed, was a warped attempt at solidarity with the Kenyan people, clumsily wielded to make a point about empathy, race and sympathy after the Paris attacks. It was telling that the BBC trending team noted that when the attack happened in April of that year, the reception of social media was utterly lacking lustre. The resurfacing of this story in order to elicit grief – or to guilt others who were already grieving – in order to make a point, was nothing but shallow, performative anti-racism. To put it bluntly, Kenyans needed that solidarity, and those social-media shares, back in April. They didn't need it seven months later, in November, as an act of self-important 'proof' that people in the UK and US care deeply about black and brown countries affected by terrorism in light of press coverage of the Paris attacks. The events in Kenya were cynically used so that people in the UK and US could prove to themselves and to their friends that they were socially aware. That they were one of the good ones. That they believed that black lives matter.[lii]

The sharing of the Garissa attack, according to Eddo-Lodge was emblematic of a somewhat fraudulent attempt by liberals to appear concerned with the loss of black lives, as much as white lives. Still, until now, there is disparity in the way that attacks against 'white' populations are reported and memorialised, as opposed to those victims of terrorism in the Middle East, the Asian Sub-Continent and Africa.

In June 2017, Facebook allowed for individuals to mark themselves as 'safe' after the London Bridge attacks, but made no such facility available for those in Tehran after an ISIS attack on the Parliamentary building. There are, of course, many more attacks occurring weekly in the Muslim world, as Muslims are targeted at a much higher frequency – 72% of attacks in

2016 having taken place in Iraq, Afghanistan, Pakistan, Nigeria and Syria, according to the Global Terrorism Index.[liii] Yet it is a blatant truth that the public displays of grief and solidarity are largely reserved for lives lost in the 'West'.

Putting aside the lie of liberal concern, there is something else in this associating. Yes, we can all sympathise with the suffering of others, and yes we should, but perhaps it is only natural that we share a special affinity to those to whom we are in closer proximity. Without a doubt, the attacks in London impacted me more than the attacks in Paris. This is not because I could not sympathise with those in Paris, but rather because there is something more potent about violence when it is closer to home.

In this respect, Islam is perhaps far more straightforward about its relationship structure. Muslims share an affinity to one another that is very much formed by a union called the umma, the body of Muslims who share love, concern and solidarity based on their shared faith. In many ways, this relationship subverts the traditional way that communities conceive of relationships. The story of Noah, as presented in the Qur'ān, is one example of how Noah was promised by Allāh that his family would be saved from the impending flood. After the flood came and Noah's son drowned, he called to Allāh by asking Him about their agreement, only for Allāh to explain to Noah that his son was not from his 'family'. The redefined relationship can be seen elsewhere, where the wife of Pharaoh refuses to believe in him as a god, Abraham smashes the idols that his father worships and the wife of Lot is condemned with her people. For Muslims, there is no concept of righteousness that is based on blood or tribe, everything comes back to belief and action. In the chapter al-Baqarah, an exchange between Abraham and Allāh highlights how this is the case:

> *And [mention, O Muḥammad], when Abraham*
> *was tried by his Lord with commands and he*
> *fulfilled them. [Allāh] said, "Indeed, I will make*
> *you a leader for the people." [Abraham] said,*
> *"And of my descendants?" [Allāh] said, "My*
> *covenant does not include the wrongdoers."[liv]*

In my life the umma has been ever present. As a child I was aware of much of what was going on in the Muslim world, even in the days when my parents and our family did not much care for religion or politics. Causes such as that of Palestine, Bosnia, Iraq and Afghanistan were somewhere in our consciousness, a connection shared in particular to suffering. It is difficult to describe this to those who do not share the feeling; they simply ask why would you feel such a close connection to those you have never met? Travelling around much of the Muslim world over the last fifteen years, I have prayed in mosques in the most remote corners, and without fail, the most destitute of them will see the imam put up his hands in prayer during Ramadan, and ask Allāh to ease the suffering of the Palestinian people. Often these people are suffering themselves, but they never fail to ask Allāh's assistance for others. This is the how Muslims internalise and externalise the well recorded tradition of the Prophet:

> *The Muslims are like a single man. If the eye is*
> *afflicted, then the whole body is afflicted. If the*
> *head is afflicted, then the whole body is*
> *afflicted.[lv]*

The umma has implications for me as a Muslim, not just within the realm of having an ethical concern, but more than that as something that has legal and political implications. Considering the world we live in, I am increasingly convinced that it is not traditional Islamic authority (Caliphate) that I am seeking, but rather a transcendental connection to the umma that allows me to still interact with other Muslims, despite them living under the despotism of kingships or other forms of authoritarian or quite frankly incompetent rule. The centrality of the umma in many ways is summarised perfectly by Dr Ovamir Anjum, who writes:

> *To begin with, the use of the word "political" with respect to the caliphate discourse must be seen as merely conventional, for it is not the good of the polis but of the Muslim Community – the umma – that the contributors to that discourse contemplated. We cannot easily brush aside differences between polis and umma, between, on the one hand, a territorially defined community that seeks the good life in this-worldly pursuits of material prosperity and intellectual enlightenment and, on the other, an ideologically defined community (with territorial unity mostly taken for granted) that seeks the ultimate good in the eternal afterlife and sees this life as only a means...[lvi]*

As a Muslim, the polis cannot capture the entirety of my concerns, and so how can I understand the world that I live in today, particularly when I have been born and raised in a country that has a minority Muslim population? It is precisely this question that Professor Salman Sayyid seeks to interrogate in his 'Recalling the Caliphate'. He starts by taking Sayyid Qutb's formulation that there is no such thing as a nationality outside of Islam, and then proceeds to determine the boundaries of such a declaration within the enduring confines of the nation state:

> *The notion of diaspora that I am advocating for the ummah is not based on racialised notions of ethnicity (in the form of a common descent from an originary homeland or ancestor), nor is it merely metaphoric in the sense of trying to come*

to terms with the mismatch between peoples and places. I do not make the claim that Muslim identity is organic, but I do argue that for various reasons it is the subject position that currently has greater prominence than other forms of identification for those who describe themselves or are described by others as Muslims.

...

The inability of the ummah to fully articulate itself as universal means that it is caught in the logic of diaspora. The ummah interrupts and prevents the nation from finding closure and, at the same time, it points to another nation that will come into being at some point in the future. In this, the ummah is a becoming—it is a horizon as well as an actuality.[lvii]

This is a hard reality for non-Muslims (and even for some Muslims) to face. They cannot understand how and why Muslims will assert a sense of affiliation that subverts the accepted norms of nation statehood – equally surprising as of course none question that international affinity that some Jewish people in the diaspora have to the state of Israel. Some Muslim commentators suggest that there is nothing wrong with Muslims being concerned with the injustices being perpetrated against other Muslims abroad, but to hold ones identity to the umma before their identity of being British, is indicative of being an 'Islamist extremist'.[lviii] For neo-conservative commentators, such as Michael Gove, he sees the connection between the politics of the umma and domestic politics as being part and parcel of the same 'problem' of Muslim identity, in his 'Celsius 7/7', he writes:

The MCB [Muslim Council of Britain] and

MAB [Muslim Association of Britain] champion the rights of terrorist suspects in Guantanamo Bay and individuals who wish to dress in a fundamentalist fashion and then complain that Muslim identity is viewed through the prism of the War on Terror and refracted by perceptions of religious extremism.[lix]

I personally do not ascribe to the dichotomy of British or Muslim – there are parts of my character and identity that are innately British and Britain is my home. However, there are parts of my Muslim identity that are non-negotiable.

My argument with Muslims who parrot government narratives about 'Islamist extremism' is not so much around the fact that they do not think the umma should have a central place in Muslim identity. Rather, it is more that they do not question the nation state, nationalism (read jingoism), the system, the establishment, capitalism, neo-liberalism, as being central to arguments around disaffection.

I would much rather live in an ethical UK, than a despotic Muslim-majority country. Islam is important to me, and spirituality more generally, so of course I would like to see that practised within public life. Whatever you call a Muslim polity, whether it is a Caliphate, or Imamate, ultimately it is unjust unless it opens itself to checks and balances and accountability processes. In his 2016 lecture at the School of Oriental and African Studies, Professor Jonathan AC Brown presented the topic 'Is there Justice Outside of God's Law?' where he explained that throughout history, Muslim scholars have not just been focused on applying the letter of the law strictly, but have consistently engaged in exercises to ensure that justice is found in a world that is ever changing.[lx]

Authoritarianism is not supposed to be normal. I

apply this same policy to my critique of democracy as a system (something I will look at more closely in the next chapter), for without accountability and the rule of law, it has all the hallmarks of repression.

Much of my thinking is about looking backwards. As I think of other instances of the past, I think to Muslims who transcended their national boundaries – whose fame took them beyond the identity of national politics, where their celebrity and myth entered the popular imagination of Muslims all over the world. When I think of such a figure, the first name that comes to mind is not an Islamic scholar or thinker, but rather a sportsman, Muḥammad Ali. Ali, who spent his early years as a Muslim within the fringe group known as the Nation of Islam, came to become the most recognised Muslim in the world. Mike Marqusee's excellent history of the period of black civil rights struggle through the lens of Muḥammad Ali provides an interesting vignette into how Ali's persona and religion entered into Muslim imagining among British-Pakistani Muslim communities in the UK:

> *Soon we were sharing common enthusiasms for the city of Lahore, for the late-swinging yorkers of Waqar Younis, for the hills outside Islamabad and for the high-grade black charas of the Himalayas. Somehow the talk turned to Muhammad Ali and a reverent hush came over our group. With a flickering smile, as if remembering something distant yet intimate, something that could never be taken from him, Akram told us how in 1966 his father, a Punjabi-speaking immigrant, took him to see Ali fight Henry Cooper at the Arsenal in Highbury.*

> *Boxing plays little part in the sporting cultures of South Asia, and Akram's father had never*

expressed an interest in it before Ali arrived in London. But he splashed out for the tickets (in those days there were still affordable seats at big-time boxing matches) because Ali was a Muslim, and because he was going to give the English- man Cooper a thrashing. For the young Akram, however, Ali was from the beginning more than an Islamic hero. He was also an ambassador of black America, the embodiment of the bewitching African-American style, as well as of black political defiance. His relevance to the young black cricketers of today's East End, who seek entry to the level playing field on their own terms and without abandoning their own identities, was obvious.

I find this passage remarkable for many reasons. It centralises Muhammad Ali's status as an icon of Islam, as a hero for Muslims, but also locates that identity within the domestic and foreign policy concerns of those Muslims. These were not 'Islamist extremists' as the accusation is levelled against Muslims of today, they were economic migrants who rarely had time for religion, but they understood repression, racism, and immoral wars. In Ali, they found a Muslim who was able to not only articulate their concerns outside of the ring, but symbolically defeat all opponents inside it.

Circling back to my interrogations at the beginning of this chapter, there is a sense that I as a member of a community – an umma – that places not only responsibilities on me towards my fellow Muslims, but also to my fellow countrymen, then I must find an identity that makes a contribution for all. In this sense, my first concern when I started my work defending those unlawfully detained at Guantanamo Bay in 2003, was that justice must be at the centre of my identity.

This didn't not spring out of the blue, for it had been something on my mind for quite some time, ever since I read John Locke's 'Second Treatise on Civil Government', in which he wrote:

> *The state of nature is governed by a law that creates obligations for everyone. And reason, which is that law, teaches anyone who takes the trouble to consult it, that because we are all equal and independent, no-one ought to harm anyone else in his life, health, liberty, or possessions.*[lxi]

I found this to be particularly remarkable at the time, because it was a formulation I was very familiar with, except that formulation was in Islam. The aims and objectives of the Islamic law, al-maqasid al-shari'a, have a formulation that pre-dates, and yet is almost perfectly replicated by Locke, that the shar'ia came to protect humans in the life, liberty, intellect, honour, religion and possessions. The similarity of these positions should not be considered something strange, for there is a transcendental quality of justice that should be evident, even where despotism or liberal authoritarianism reigns.

So I come to my point, that I am less concerned with that exact nature of the political system, as much as I am about its ability to have checks and balances, good governance, and processes of accountability. These are some of the cornerstones of just societies, and it is they that will ultimately be successful.

But we don't need to reinvent the wheel. This sentiment has been captured by the fourteenth century scholar of Islam, Shaykh-ul-Islam ibn Taymiyya:

> *Human welfare in matters of this world can be attained more with justice that is accompanied by sins (other than injustice) than with injustice in matters of people's rights even if that does not*

accompany (any other) sins. That is why it has been said: God establishes a just state (dawla), be it unbelieving, but does not establish an unjust state, be it Muslim. It is also said: (the affairs of) this world can last with justice and unbelief but cannot last with injustice and Islam. The Apostle of God, peace and blessings be upon him, has said in the same vein: "No sin is quicker in divine chastisement than usurpation of other's rights (baghy) and severance of family ties." The usurper is punished in this very world, even if he might be forgiven in the Hereafter, for justice is the principle (nizam) of everything. Thus, inasmuch as its affairs are based on justice, a state will persist even if its rulers have no share in the Hereafter (due to their lack of faith); and if justice is absent, it will not persist, even if its rulers are rewarded in the Hereafter for their faith.[lxii]

Injustice cannot persist. Of this I am sure, although the world around me conspires to suggest otherwise. I am no longer as cynical as I used to be though. In the past I would see inaction by itself as the sole cause of injustice, which is still true to a great extent. However, when I think back to the Prophetic narration that whoever cannot change a wrongdoing with their hand, should speak against it with their tongue, and if they are unable to do that, then they should hate that wrongdoing in their heart – I now know that even the hating in the heart is a positive action. It means that the hearts are alive, that there is a common beat from which we can collectively work.

Who is to bring this change though? When I speak about collectively, it is very much with the notion in mind that there are glaring inadequacies in the way that we operate. In 2006 I wrote a lengthy essay 'O Brother Where Art Thou?' interviewing activists from four different prominent Muslim rights organisations. All of my interviews were with Muslim women, largely because it is women who were at the front of these organisations. Whenever I would attend a demonstration, speak at an event or attend a meeting, it was women who were doing the heavy lifting. I found out that Muslim women were travelling across London carrying heavy tables in order to set up stalls, sleeping only 3 hours a night to deal with xyz, and undertaking interactions they found personally uncomfortable but felt no one else would do it, because for them, the jump from sympathy to empathy to action seemed to be far easier to make. One of the women I spoke to, Sumayyah, described the difficulty of balancing her various obligations:

> *Although I try my best to give my children their rights and reduce my work in their waking hours, and devote that time to them, at times, I still have to apologise to them. I say sorry with tears in my eyes and explain that the Muslims are being oppressed, and that I am trying to help them, that Mama has to do that because there are too few people who will do it; that one day I hope they will understand. I ask them to be patient with me and that Allāh will give them jannah for their patience.*[lxiii]

I wondered about this disparity in the Muslim activist scene – recognising there could be multiple reasons for it. Like I mentioned in my 2006 article, I am not in the place to determine the boundaries of right and wrong, this will always be a matter for those more learned in Islamic sciences than I am, but there is no denying that while we praise women for playing some roles, they are not being recognised for the other contributions they make. Even then, it is difficult for women to play these roles, despite their desire to do so, sometimes at personal cost. As one of the women explained to me:

> *My father does not like me doing this. He just thinks it's a matter of making du'a, that is all we can do. He thinks things like this can get us into trouble with the authorities, etc. Where is the Tawakkul [reliance on Allāh] of the Muslims? Maybe that is one of the reasons why some sisters don't get involved, because of family, etc.*[lxiv]

We need to have conversations about how men and women play roles in facing challenges to the systemic oppression communities face. This cannot be done without giving full weight to context, but this discussion must be natural and authentic – started and lead from inside these communities with a framing that is genuine. Too often the debates around 'saving Muslim women' are securitised, and so exist in a place that is ultimately harmful to communities in the long term, as they feel their religion is being socially engineered from above. As Sara Farris writes in her book 'In the Name of Women's Rights':

> *...femocrats whose arguments converge with nationalists and neoliberals in anti-Islam campaigns as being "instrumentalized" by the latter— approach that is as patronizing to them as is the idea that Muslim women are agentless victims to be rescued. In other words, while feminism— the general notion of women's liberation from patriarchy—has certainly been opportunistically appropriated by the PW, FN, and LN in their struggle against the non-western and Muslim male Other, those feminists women's organizations, female politicians, and femocrats who have openly supported policies*

> *repressive of Muslim religious and social*
> *practices in the name of gender justice should*
> *not be considered as naïve political actors.*
> *Rather, they should be regarded as political*
> *subjects whose anti-Islam concerns are*
> *informed by specific theoretical paradigms and*
> *animated by determined motivations and*
> *goals.*[lxv]

Scholars and public figures must come together in order to provide their communities with guidance, while recognising the apathy and loss of resource that might have taken root in one section of our communities, and the eagerness and contribution that is increasingly available in the other.

As witnesses to the world we live in, we have responsibilities to not just be bystanders. We most move through the ranks. We must, to borrow from Maya Angelou, rise. We need to take that feeling in the heart and have the conviction to take it to our tongue, but then further than that, to have the strength to change it with our hands.

What we must never do is to permit that flickering feeling in the heart, to deaden, to rot away until not only do we become bystanders, but also we become collaborators with that oppression. In the next chapter, I will seek to think about the complexity of this further.

Our witness must be one of action. We must be like the Children of Israel who spoke, not like those who were in on the wrong or those who remained silent – they are our example. The sh-h-d root in the Arabic language is about witnessing, and the ultimate manifestation of that witness is the shaheed - the one who is martyred – the one who witnessed not just in his life, but through his death.

A Matter of 'Representation'

"One must lie low, no matter how much it went against the grain, and try to understand that this great organization remained, so to speak, in a state of delicate balance, and that if someone took it upon himself to alter the dispositions of things around him, he ran the risk of losing his footing and falling to destruction, while the organization would simply right itself by some compensating reaction in another part of its machinery – since everything interlocked – and remain unchanged, unless, indeed, which was very probable, it became still more rigid, more vigilant, severer, and more ruthless."
[Franz Kafka – The Trial]

"No empire imposed by force or otherwise has ever been without this feature: control of the indigenous by members of their own group. In the case of Gilead, there were many women willing to serve as Aunts, either because of a genuine belief in what they called "traditional values", or for the benefits they might thereby acquire. When power is scarce, a little of it is tempting..."
[Margaret Attwood – The Handmaid's Tale]

"These people were content with their environment, and felt no particular objection to an impersonal steel and concrete landscape, no qualms about the invasion of their privacy by government agencies and organizations, and if anything welcoming these intrusions, using them for their own purposes. These people were the first to master a new kind of 20th century life. They thrived on the rapid turnover of acquaintances, the lack of involvement with others, and the total self-sufficiency of lives which, needing nothing, were never disappointed. Alternatively, their real needs might emerge later."
[JG Ballard – High Rise]

Identity politics within African-American boxing did not begin with Muhammad Ali. In fact, sport, as a site of contestation regarding race, and the place of non-whites within public imagining was already being played out between two of America's famous black personalities. The debates between the celebrated African-American sportsmen Jackie Robinson and Paul Robeson during the black civil rights movement became central to notions of black empowerment and civic life.

Mike Marqusee described this period as essentially a battle between black men that was 'staged for white men'. In the context of the McCarthyite House of Un-American Activities, the debate was reduced to the question: where do the loyalties of black America lie? Robinson decried Paul Robeson's unhelpful attitude in holding black America 'back', especially when Robeson would say:

> *I defy any part of an insolent, dominating America, however powerful. I defy any errand boys, Uncle Toms of the Negro people, to challenge my Americanism because by word and deed I challenge this vicious system to the death. I'm looking for freedom, full freedom, not an inferior brand...We do not want to die in vain any more on foreign battlefields for Wall Street and the greedy supporters of domestic fascism. If we must die, let it be in Mississippi or Georgia. Let it be wherever we are lynched and deprived of our rights as human beings.[lxvi]*

Jackie Robinson had been pitted as the ideal black man due to his condemnation of those he considered to be 'extremist' in their condemnation of 'white' America. None of this was to any avail; after J Edgar Hoover launched his Counter-Intelligence Program (COINTELPRO) in August 1967, Robinson was included as a 'dangerous black nationalist'. Later, Robinson came to agree with the positions that had been put forward by Robeson:

> *In those days I had more faith in the ultimate justice of the American white man than I have today. I would reject such an invitation if offered now... I have grown wiser and closer to painful truths about America's destructiveness, and I do have increased respect for Paul Robeson who for over twenty years sacrificed himself, his career and the wealth and comfort he once enjoyed because, I believe, he was sincerely trying to help his people.[lxvii]*

This wasn't the first time that the black civil rights movement in the US had encountered schisms in approaches by recognised or leading figures. In his stunning portrayal and reflections on life for black people in the US, W.E.B. du Bois reserved some of his most stinging criticism for Booker T. Washington in 'The Souls of Black Folk'. Du Bois recognised that Washington emerged as a public figure, largely due to the need of white society to find a broker so that the, "voice of criticism was hushed" and the general acceptance of the black person as being inferior.[lxviii] He is, however, careful not to alienate Washington completely (and perhaps in his own way wrongly so):

> *If worse come to worst, can the moral fibre of this country survive the slow throttling and murder of nine millions of men? The black men of America have a duty to perform, a duty stern and delicate,--a forward movement to oppose a part of the work of their greatest leader. So far as Mr. Washington preaches Thrift, Patience, and Industrial Training for the masses, we must hold up his hands and strive with him, rejoicing in his honors and glorying in the strength of*

> *this Joshua called of God and of man to lead the*
> *headless host. But so far as Mr. Washington*
> *apologizes for injustice, North or South, does*
> *not rightly value the privilege and duty of*
> *voting, belittles the emasculating effects of caste*
> *distinctions, and opposes the higher training*
> *and ambition of our brighter minds,––so far as*
> *he, the South, or the Nation, does this,––we*
> *must unceasingly and firmly oppose them.[lxix]*

Booker T.Washington's role as a gatekeeper for black society in America was an important role. He attempted to alleviate the suffering of some of his people, but what W.E.B. du Bois helped us to ask is, at what cost? I am reminded of another Booker T...except this one is from the world of the World Wrestling Federation (WWF later WWE), where one of the black celebrity wrestlers had taken the name of his forebear for the stage. Although not a 'bad' character within the world of WWF, he was an underdog, but key to note, is that Booker T was consistently denied a narrative of success, even when he came to his closest moment against the 'bad' character of Triple-H – the archetypal bad guy who (was white) somehow always ended up on top:

> *There's real-life drama and then there's*
> *fictional drama. WWE's response to allegations*
> *of racism, misogyny, homophobia, and ableism*
> *have always been the same: It's fictional. But*
> *that excuse wears thin when the fictional racism*
> *lines up perfectly with the real-life racism.*
>
> *Triple H the character said somebody like*
> *Booker T doesn't get to be a champion, and he*
> *was right. Nobody like Booker T has ever been*
> *WWE's world champion. For whatever reason,*
> *WWE's decision makers decided that Booker T,*
> *and every black athlete before him and after*

> *him, is not the kind of guy they want as the*
> *representative of their company.*[lxx]

These debates resonate with me greatly as I think about Muslim life in the UK. We are often told that the panacea to disenfranchisement and alienation of communities, is representation – that by Muslims being represented in politics, the media, the police force (even WWE) and other institutions, that this will inevitably result in a correcting of biases against our communities. In another art form, that of rap, even the very critical Tupac Shakur was not immune to call of 'representation', in his song 'Changes', he rapped:

> *And although it seems heaven sent,*
> *we ain't ready to see a black President,*
> *It ain't a secret don't conceal the fact...*
> *the penitentiary's packed, and it's filled with*
> *blacks.*
> *But some things will never change.*[lxxi]

As with the Robinson/Robeson debate, issues of representation are not new. Tupac sang of the need for a black president as a panacea to the problems of black America – seemingly beyond possibility to the extent it would need to be 'heaven sent'. He linked this lack of political-representation to the endemic problem of over-representation of black men in the penal system of America. This is only part of the problem, and perhaps it was Obama's presidency that finally gave truth to the lie that 'representation' can save us from the situation we currently find ourselves in, as the 'system' is something much larger than the limited scope of our particular concerns. Naomi Klein summarises the meaninglessness of representation politics in her new book 'No Is Not Enough' when she says:

> *It's worth remembering that a large portion of*
> *Barack Obama's base was quite happy to*

embrace the carefully crafted symbols his administration created – the White House lit up like a rainbow to celebrate gay marriage; the shift to civil, erudite tone; the spectacle of an incredibly appealing first family free of major scandals for eight years. And these were all good things. But, too often, these same supporters looked the other way when it came to the drone warfare that killed countless civilians, or the deportations of roughly 2.5 million immigrants without documents during Obama's term, or his broken promises to close Guantanamo or shut down George W. Bush's mass-surveillance architecture. Obama positioned himself as a climate hero, but at one point bragged that his administration had "added enough new oil and gas pipelines to encircle the Earth and then some.[lxxii]

The criticisms that Naomi Klein mentions of Barack Obama were not lost in other contexts. Assata Shakur relates how her early life was very much dictated by notions of class emancipation – it was not just race that played a factor, class and economics featured significantly in what it meant to grow up in an environment of disenfranchisement:

Although my grandmother taught me more about being proud and strong than anyone I know, she had a lot of Booker T. Washington, pull yourself up by the bootstraps, "talented tenth" ideas. She had worked hard and had made a decent living as a pieceworker in a factory, but she had other ideas for me. She was determined that I would become part of Wilmington's talented tenth – the privileged class – part of the so-called Black bourgeoisie.[lxxiii]

Today I look at Muslim politicians, and most of them do not particularly represent Muslim interests, although occasionally they do. If we take the notion of representation as our guide, then by that standard the current opposition leader Jeremy Corbyn far better 'represents' Muslim concerns than many Muslim parliamentarians.

The Robinson/Robeson and Washington/DuBois debates are instructive, as they tell me that there is a layer that exists that is beyond our reach, beyond our ability to change, and that the discussions around resistance and representation that we are having, are largely restricted to our own immediate concerns, and not in relation to longer and wider reaching notions of transcendental justice.

Robinson was lauded for his role by the McCarthyite lobby, he represented the best of being a reconciled African-American, one who was not willing to challenge the status quo but rather encourage his communities to take advantage of the opportunities they had been given. Unfortunately for Robinson, this did not stop the FBI considering him a 'dangerous black nationalist', and neither did it stop his eventual disappointment with being failed by the system.

The System

What is the system though? In this chapter I want to understand the structure that we are dealing with, and explore how notions of representation and loyalty play a role in the way that I understand my relationship with authority. Further, I want to understand how I interact with those who choose a different path from me within my community. So often the debate becomes black and white, and so if there are red lines, where are they and how do I engage with people on the other side of them? First, we need to acknowledge that where we are does not exist in a vacuum – it is the inevitable conclusion of a process that preceded the horrifying election of Donald J Trump or the British referendum calling for a Brexit from the European Union. Naomi Klein situates Trump in his correct context:

> ...*Trump, extreme as he is, is less an aberration than a logical conclusion – a pastiche of pretty much all the worst trends of the past half century. Trump is the product of powerful systems of thought that rank human life based on race, religion, gender, sexuality, physical appearance, and physical ability – and that have systematically used race as a weapon to advance brutal economic policies since the earliest days of North American colonization and the trans-Atlantic slave trade.* [lxxiv]

Going to back to the first of my questions at the start of this section, I want to know in what environment I am operating – and as a consequence of asking this question, want to have the means of assessing whether or not the playing field even provides enough enticement to enter the pitch or indeed, the system. Perhaps, in my opinion, one of the most eloquent descriptions of the system from the perspective of race, and the way that it can structurally discriminate is by Reni Eddo-Lodge:

> *The covert nature of structural racism is difficult to hold to account. It slips out of your hands easily like a water-snake toy. You can't spot it as easily as a St George's flag and a bare belly at an English Defence League march. It's much more respectable than that.*
>
> *I appreciate that the word structural can feel and sound abstract. Structural. What does that even mean? I choose to use the word structural*

> *rather than institutional because I think it is built into spaces much broader than our more traditional institutions. Thinking of the big picture helps you see the structures. Structural racism is dozens, or hundreds, or thousands of people with the same biases joining together to make up one organisation, and acting accordingly. Structural racism is an impenetrably white workplace culture set by those people, where anyone who falls outside of the culture must conform or face failure. Structural is often the only way to capture what goes unnoticed - the silently raised eyebrows, the implicit biases, snap judgements made on perceptions of competency.*[lxxv]

What Eddo-Lodge is referring to is the everyday low-level aggressions against black and minority ethnic communities in the UK. Through studies, we know that those with African, Arab or Asian names are more likely to be refused a job interview despite having comparable experience and education to 'white' job seekers. These are not old arguments by those who are critical of the structure of racism – W.E.B. du Bois had correctly identified how the law itself served to harm black communities in the US:

> *Daily the Negro is coming more and more to look upon law and justice, not as protecting safeguards, but as sources of humiliation and oppression. The laws are made by men who have little interest in him; they are executed by men who have absolutely no motive for treating the black people with courtesy or consideration; and, finally, the accused law-breaker is tried, not by his peers, but too often by men who would rather punish ten innocent Negroes than let one guilty one escape.*[lxxvi]

The more I reflect and interact with other communities, the more I realise what structural racism means. It means that for people of colour, access to employment, housing, medical care and social welfare have prejudices built in as hurdles. This is not, by any means, a level playing field. At a conference I attended at Birkbeck College in London on 'Resisting the (Internal) Borders'. I listened as activists and scholars spoke of how migrants and people of colour were systematically discriminated against, so that in order to be able to access treatment in the UK, they would need to allow their health to deteriorate to the level of an emergency. This cannot stand! How can we even think that a world should exist where humans are having to surrender to such considerations?

'The System' is not just one 'thing', it is an entire mode of knowledge production and narrative formation that works interdependently to reinforce the power of authority, over the bodies and minds of the disenfranchised. Writing a new preface to his 1970s book 'Orientalism', Edward W Said re-examined the significance of his work in light of the US invasion of Iraq in 2003, and how all elements of the state colluded to permit such levels of unlawful violence:

> *The major influences on George W. Bush's Pentagon and National Security Council were men such as Bernard Lewis and Fouad Ajami, experts on the Arab and Islamic world who helped the American hawks to think about such preposterous phenomena as the Arab mind and centuries-old Islamic decline that only American power could reverse. Today, bookstores in the US are filled with shabby screeds bearing screaming headlines about Islam and terror, Islam exposed, the Arab threat and the Muslim menace, all of them written by*

> *political polemicists pretending to knowledge imparted to them and others by experts who have supposedly penetrated to the heart of these strange Oriental peoples over there who have been such a terrible thorn in "our" flesh. Accompanying such warmongering expertise have been the omnipresent CNNs and Foxs of this world, plus myriad numbers of evangelical and right-wing radio hosts, plus innumerable tabloids and even middle-brow journalists, all of them re-cycling the same unverifiable fictions and vast generalizations so as to stir up "America" against the foreign devil.[lxxvii]*

I was also devastated to learn that according to the geographer Danny Dorling, racism is so endemic within the system, that, "the majority of children who live above the fourth floor of tower blocks, in England, are black or Asian." [lxxviii]So as I sit here, writing less than a week after the Grenfell Towers in the Royal Borough of Kensington and Chelsea have burnt down, with it seems, at the time of this writing, that at least eighty people died in the fire, with hundreds more displaced.[lxxix]

This is the structurally racist system – one that cares more for the superficial looks of a building for the sake of wealthier residents in the area, than for the safety of those that live inside. At this moment of writing, I am still haunted by the videos and audio clips of those who spent their last moments calling loved ones, seeking forgiveness, making prayers, losing hope with the world and turning to help in the Almighty. With Grenfell Tower, I am reminded of JG Ballard's 'High Rise':

> *In a sense life in the high-rise had begun to resemble the world outside - there were the same ruthlessness and aggression concealed*

within a set of polite conventions.

These polite conventions are the ones that mask the everyday racism that allows for the destruction of black and brown lives. Nothing says this to me more than the news I received the day after the Grenfell fire, that Jeronimo Yanez, a police officer from Minnesota was acquitted of unlawfully killing Philando Castile – a young black man who was, for any fair minded thinking person, killed unlawfully. The video is testimony that there is absolutely no doubt this was the case.

This is how the 'system' works interdependently, reinforcing the notion that those in power are subject to a degree of benefit-of-the-doubt that simply does not exist for people of colour. The reverence for police who are the very force on trial permeates the courtroom proceedings, the justice system itself. The prosecution claims that they have to be measured how they speak about the police, the judge is reliant on the police for protection, and the jury considers the police to be responsible for keeping them safe from the very people the police kill – it's a fix.

It is telling for me, that in response to the verdict of not-guilty for Yanez, Castile's sister Allysza said:

I will never have faith in the system.[lxxx]

Perhaps because she meant to, or perhaps she didn't realise, but she located the verdict, the trial, the court, both prosecution and defence, within the system, one that cannot be trusted with the equal care of black lives.

Philando Castile's life mattered, because HE mattered, as does every single human being. When we say Black Lives Matter, it is because we know that in the 'system' black lives matter less than other lives. I do not shout Black Lives Matter for the sake of the preservation of brown lives or Muslim lives, but because I know that black lives matter for their own sake – we must change our optics to be aware of that.

The Grenfell Tower fire and the verdict in the Philando Castile case felt like two very hard hits to take. In the early hours of those last Ramadan nights in 2017, I was stopped in my writing by the news of 17-year-old Nabra Hassanen having been murdered by two attackers, with 22-year-old Darwin Martinez Torres charged with the offence.

From what we know of the story so far during a break from night prayers, Hassanen went with friends to McDonalds to eat, only to be attacked by two men with baseball bats. While the friends managed to escape, she was kidnapped and beaten to death. The visibility of Muslim women, who wear the hijab out of a personal sense of devotion, means they are the most visible manifestation of Islam today. A Muslim man with a beard could pass as a hipster. Yes, the hijab is something women choose to wear out of a sense of obligation, and so cannot be directly equated to black skin, but it is still an overt symbol of who they are, and so they are readily recognisable, and therefore targetable. I mourn for this soul who is lost to us in such extreme violence – nothing can compensate – and yet we pray that Allāh grants her the martyrdom she deserves, a witness to the hate that is directed against Muslim lives, as we become witnesses to her loss.

The idea that some lives are worth more than others is perhaps best exemplified by the reality that there is both different treatment and a different lens through which lives taken are written or spoken about. The inexplicable killing of Justine Diamond, a 40-year-old white Australian woman living in Minneapolis, US provided an interesting juxtaposition to the way in which the killing of black lives is covered. Not only was there international interest in the case, but within a week of the killing the Minneapolis police chief Janee

Harteau had resigned as a quick act of accountability. This type of response has not been seen in any of the other cases of black lives being killed by police officers, highlighting again the extent to which lives are not only unequally reported, but also responded to.[lxxxi] In an environment where the police have closed ranks through social media campaigns such as #BlueLivesMatter as a response to accountability requests for police shootings, it is worth reflecting on the words of Eduardo Bonilla-Silva in his 'Racism without Racists':

> *...whites enunciate positions to safeguard their racial interests without sounding "racist". Shielded by color blindness, whites can express their resentment toward minorities; criticize their morality, and work ethic, even claim to be victims of "reverse racism*[lxxxii]

One of the first books I read at the very beginning of 2017, was the account of Trayvon Martin's killing, written by his parents Tracy Martin and Sybrina Fulton, 'Rest in Power'. The account, of a couple who are no longer together, responding to the news in their own ways and coming together over the loss of their son is something that is profound on many levels. George Zimmerman, the man who killed Trayvon Martin, was ultimately acquitted of any crime. The jury accepted that he was in his rights to think he was in danger.

But how did George Zimmerman come to think of Martin as posing a threat? To understand that, we need to understand everything that I have written above. We need to pause and think about how the everyday fear and bigotry of individuals metastasises into both direct and indirect forms of discrimination. In the case of Trayvon Martin, this resulted in his unlawful and untimely execution. The key piece of evidence that I wish to rely on, is what Zimmerman told the police detective Serino at the police station:

> *"Okay, but as far as identifying people and stuff like that, as far as what to look for..."*
>
> *The killer told him that there had been a PowerPoint presentation at a neighborhood watch event.*
>
> *"Okay, I wasn't privy to that," said Serino. "But if you guys continue neighborhood watch, typically speaking at night time the [criminal] garb is black on black with a black hoodie. Now, this guy had a dark gray hoodie. It was dark but his pants were beige. Not quite your [sic], you know, prime suspect type."*
>
> *After a discussion of previous burglary in the community, and what the shooter said Trayvon was doing on the night he was killed, Serino said, "You know you are going to come under a lot of scrutiny over this, correct? Okay, the profiling aspect of the whole thing. Had this person been white, would you have felt the same way?" "Yes," he said.*[lxxxiii]

First, based on the full narrative of the way he confronted Trayvon Martin, I question his sincerity that he would have acted in the same way to a white person in a hoodie. Regardless, he understood the signs to look out for...from a PowerPoint presentation. A neighbourhood watch event taught him how to spot the signs of danger, by giving profiling tips, in a predominantly white area. The inherent bigotry that goes into making these judgements provided all the wrong type of information, which then coalesced in a scared and cowardly individual in the form of George Zimmerman, someone who would rather place his fear of others before doing the right thing. It is presentations such as these that have their roots in the anthropology of genocide, in the stereotyping of communities in order to specifically assess their threat levels – and ultimately – they are all reductive with overwhelming consequences.

The PowerPoint (or slideshow) that leads to discrimination is particularly relevant in my world of challenging counter-terrorism policies in the UK. In 2015, the UK government brought into law the Counter-Terrorism and Security Act. This piece of legislation made it a statutory duty for all public sector workers to report those under their care who might exhibit signs of 'radicalisation', under the auspices of the Prevent strategy – designed to stop future acts of violence in what the government calls the 'pre-crime' space.

This applies to health care professionals such as doctors, nurses, dentists and opticians; education sector professionals such as university lecturers, teachers, nursery teachers and even child-minders; but of course the public sector is much wider, and so applies to anyone who is in a position to represent both government or local authority. The training that is given to these public sector workers, is a three-hour PowerPoint presentation where they are taught about the 22+ factors of radicalisation that they should look out for. These factors include:

1. *Grievance/injustice*

2. *Threat*

3. *Identity, meaning and belonging*

4. *Status*

5. *Excitement, comradeship or adventure*

6. *Dominance and control*

7. Susceptibility to indoctrination

8. Political/moral motivation

9. Opportunistic involvement

10. Family and/or friends support extremist offending

11. Transitional periods

12. Group influence and control

13. Mental health

14. Over-identification with a group, cause or ideology

15. Them and Us thinking

16. Dehumanisation of the enemy

17. Attitudes that justify offending

18. Harmful means to an end

19. Harmful objectives

20. Individual knowledge, skills and competencies

21. Access to networks, funding or equipment for terrorism

22. Criminal capability[lxxxiv]

For even those with a cursory knowledge of threat detection, these factors tell teachers very little about how to spot threats. Children could feel a sense of grievance over many issues, and even desire moral or political change, but to suggest that teachers, of all people – those who should be nurturing and encouraging critical thinking and a desire for a better society in children - should be trained with such guidance is unconscionable.

The vagueness of the terms is bad enough, but then when this is coupled with an individual's taught or own anxiety about certain communities, it inevitably leads to a culture of over reporting. Particularly when the legislation states that those public sector workers who fail to comply with the guidance, will be taken to court to enforce the legislation's use. This is how the structural racism of the state is established, so that even those who may not agree with government policy, are drawn into its implementation through the enactment of laws. As Hannah Arendt remarked in the Eichmann case, this is the 'banality of evil'[lxxxv].

I want to draw a line between the PowerPoint that was used to educate George Zimmerman and the slides that are used to educate public sector workers in the UK. The logics and conclusions of these presentations are the same: that future violence can be predicted based on specific types of profiles that are presented as common sense. Except they are not. They are based on bigoted understandings and ultimately racist assumptions.

When we have a child in the UK, who wears a t-shirt with Abu Bakr al-Siddiq (the first Caliph of Islam) written on the back, who is reported to the authorities for being a supporter of Abu Bakr al-Baghdadi (the leader of ISIS), then this is just one example out of the thousands of individuals who have been referred through misunderstandings and fear of Islam. Perhaps more significant, is those who have been cooperating with the Prevent programme, having themselves been profiled. In 2016, Faiza Shaheen was pulled off an airplane for reading a book on Syrian artwork. As someone who involved herself with a programme of 'early identification' through the Prevent policy, she recognised the potential for it to go wrong:

I have always felt cautious making judgments

> *on cases around radicalisation, but this*
> *experience has made me more aware of the*
> *regrettable scar it can leave on people when a*
> *misjudgment is made. Singling out people in*
> *this way could cause, for certain individuals,*
> *quite a detrimental effect to their overall*
> *wellbeing.*[lxxxvi]

Similarly in April 2017, a Muslim youth-worker who regularly works with Prevent officials was arrested under terrorism laws over suspicion that a family holiday to Turkey was an attempt to join ISIS.[lxxxvii] I want to return to some of the data around these referrals in the next chapter, but for now it is enough that we have a conversation around how subjective assessments allow for abuses to occur.

I want our communities to understand that there is a structural form of racism that exists, pervades and perpetuates. It floats between communities as it finds new life in targeting the latest community to present a threat. Currently, conversations around the 'threat' posed by Muslims, is entirely indicative of the ways in which counter-terrorism policy has formed as part of the structural discrimination taking place against Muslims today. In the words of Narzanin Massoumi, Tom Mills and David Miller in their book highlighting the racism of anti-Muslim hatred 'What is Islamophobia?":

> *We regard the state, and more specifically the*
> *sprawling official 'counter-terrorism'*
> *apparatus, to be absolutely central to*
> *production of contemporary Islamophobia – the*
> *backbone of anti-Muslim racism.*[lxxxviii]

This is the world that Muslims in the West occupy, one where they are problematized, stigmatised and spoken about, rather than with. Turning back to our modalities of oppression, by focusing on a very specific minority, it has been easy to demonise Muslims who have found it traditionally difficult to break out of cycles of poverty, to be 'represented', to have their voice and to be the owners of their own story. James Baldwin has a way of capturing the story of the disenfranchised in a way that many others are not able. The documentary based on his last unfinished writings 'I Am Not Your Negro' is highly revealing of the way in which narratives of oppression must be owned by the oppressed, in order to begin to understand their experience:

> *People finally say to you,*
>
> *in an attempt to dismiss the social reality, "But you're so bitter!"*
>
> *Well, I may or may not be bitter,*
>
> *but if I were, I would have good reasons for it: chief among them that American blindness,*
>
> *or cowardice, which allows us to pretend that life presents no reasons for being bitter.*[lxxxix]

As I think about the difficulty of making ourselves heard, I am reminded of the African-American actor Jessie Williams, whose speech at the Black Entertainment Television (BET) awards perfectly summarises the way in which structural racism is maintained by the system.

> *Now, this award - this is not for me. This is for the real organizers all over the country - the activists, the civil rights attorneys, the struggling parents, the families, the teachers, the students that are realizing that a system built to divide and impoverish and destroy us cannot stand if we do.*
>
> *It's kind of basic mathematics - the more we*

learn about who we are and how we got here, the more we will mobilize.

...

Now, what we've been doing is looking at the data and we know that police somehow manage to deescalate, disarm and not kill white people everyday. So what's going to happen is we are going to have equal rights and justice in our own country or we will restructure their function and ours.

Now... I got more y'all - yesterday would have been young Tamir Rice's 14th birthday so I don't want to hear anymore about how far we've come when paid public servants can pull a drive-by on 12 year old playing alone in the park in broad daylight, killing him on television and then going home to make a sandwich. Tell Rekia Boyd how it's so much better than it is to live in 2012 than it is to live in 1612 or 1712. Tell that to Eric Garner. Tell that to Sandra Bland. Tell that to Dorian Hunt.

Now the thing is, though, all of us in here getting money - that alone isn't gonna stop this. Alright, now dedicating our lives, dedicating our lives to getting money just to give it right back for someone's brand on our body when we spent centuries praying with brands on our bodies, and now we pray to get paid for brands on our bodies.

There has been no war that we have not fought and died on the front lines of. There has been no job we haven't done. There is no tax they haven't leveed [sic] against us - and we've paid all of them. But freedom is somehow always conditional here. "You're free," they keep telling us. But she would have been alive if she hadn't acted so... free.

Now, freedom is always coming in the hereafter, but you know what, though, the hereafter is a hustle. We want it now.

And let's get a couple things straight, just a little sidenote - the burden of the brutalized is not to comfort the bystander. That's not our job, alright - stop with all that. If you have a critique for the resistance, for our resistance, then you better have an established record of critique of our oppression. If you have no interest, if you have no interest in equal rights for black people then do not make suggestions to those who do. Sit down.

We've been floating this country on credit for centuries, yo, and we're done watching and waiting while this invention called whiteness uses and abuses us, burying black people out of sight and out of mind while extracting our culture, our dollars, our entertainment like oil - black gold, ghettoizing and demeaning our creations then stealing them, gentrifying our genius and then trying us on like costumes before discarding our bodies like rinds of strange fruit.[xc]

Collaborators

Williams' speech is a pathway to understanding what we mean when we talk about engagement and representation. As I mentioned earlier, representation is sold to our communities as the holy grail of acceptance. If a Muslim becomes a Member of

Parliament, he has not only achieved the highest status of representation, but also then becomes an exemplar for representation. If you look then, to those Muslim MPs who were part of Tony Blair's Labour Party, they were pro or abstained on issues to do with war, securitisation and neo-liberalism – and so when I want to consider what the panacea to structural racism and the system's inherent bias against us might look like, I remain unconvinced that it takes place through people that look, sound and have the same names as me, but whose politics are not only alien, they are a complete deformation of my commitment to social justice.

I want to know first how the Qur'ān speaks to me about representation. I think of my local Imam again, the one who yells at our congregation ad nauseam that we must obey the rulers and the agents of the state, even if they oppress us. Surely, one could take the view that these acts are a part of the corrective process of the state, that they are in fact a form of engagement with the state?

I want to consider a fringe story from the encounter between Moses and Pharaoh. These figures are marginal ones, and only make fleeting appearances in the Qur'ān, but are central to my thinking about engagement and representation. One is from the family/tribe of Pharaoh, who is known as the secret believer – we are never told his name. The other is Korah (Qarun), said to be the paternal cousin of Moses. It is a strange juxtaposition that is presented in the Qur'ān. The secret believer is related to Pharaoh, and yet despite a high status he is given in Pharaoh's advisors, he rejects the faith of his leader.

The secret believer knows he is in a precarious position. Perhaps he was a member of the ruling establishment and bore witness to all that the establishment done? Perhaps he was there when the Children of Israel were enslaved? Perhaps he was there when their children were killed. I am fascinated by him. Here is a man, who is considered to have acted in a laudatory way by Allāh, within the heart of an oppressive establishment.

In my view, he was not someone who could claim not to have witnessed the crimes that were committed, and yet, unlike those who were considered complicit, such as Pharoah's chief-of-staff Hamman and Korah, his name is hidden from us – leaving me with the feeling that sometimes the best advocates, are the ones we do not see. The ones who work against tyranny, and use their privilege in order to effect change towards good, especially when the moment comes for them to speak truth to power.

There are various accounts of who this individual is, but there is suggestion that he is a paternal cousin[xci] of Pharoah, but Ibn Abbas goes further to name him as Ezekiel[xcii]. This man hides his faith from those around him. He became a Muslim in secret and like the wife of Pharoah, worshipped Allāh privately. The key argument that is used by the man, and a phrase later invoked by the Prophet Muḥammad's best friend Abu Bakr to defend him, is, "Do you kill a man [merely] because he says, 'My Lord is Allāh.'" The idea is put into the minds of those attempting to assassinate Moses, that no actual harm has been committed by him, but rather that they are attempting to kill an idea. He goes on further to argue that should Moses be in the right, then they would bring about God's punishment on themselves, to kill him if he is lying is pointless, as he cannot harm them with words. Conversely, to kill Moses, if he is telling the truth, would be only harmful to themselves. Sayyid Qutb says of this man:

> At heart, the man feels what a true believer
> should feel: God's punishment is closest to those
> who are in power. Therefore, they are the ones

who should be most careful and should try their best to avoid it. It could come upon them at any moment of the night or day, so they must dread such a possibility. The man reminds them of the power and authority they enjoyed, and includes himself among them as he reminds them of God's punishment: "Who will rescue us from God's punishment should it befall us?" (Verse 29) He, thus, shows them that what happens to them is a matter of great concern to him; he is one of them, awaiting the same destiny.[xciii]

The secret believer is alive and present within the structure of oppression. This is difficult for me because in my mind there is a degree of complicity. So at times, the Qur'ān alludes to the fact that one may find oneself within an inner sanctum of an administration that is not only oppressive, in a real, practical sense but in an archetypal way as well.

What makes this man's actions laudable? Is it restricted to the fact that he believed in Allāh? I don't think this is the case. In my view, it is the secret believer's speaking truth to power the moment it was necessary and urgent to do so. He was not just speaking at this moment in order to do the right thing, but he identified that supporting Moses was the most utilitarian use of any proclamation. The man's cleverness is further highlighted by him not making it a matter of 'us v them', but as Sayyid Qutb reflects above, that he is one of their number, so whatever decision is made, he will share that fate.

If you are making claims to representation within the confines of authority, then the litmus test of your connection to your community is very much based on direct correlation to speaking the community's truths. Without being able to achieve this, you are another member of the machine. It is not enough that you are someone who was weak and oppressed by the administration, this is also clear from the same chapter when Allāh describes the pleas of those who did not speak out against Pharaoh:

> *A terrible punishment engulfed Pharaoh's people; they will be brought before the Fire morning and evening. On the Day the Hour comes, it will be said, 'Throw Pharaoh's people into the worst torment.' In the Fire they will quarrel with one another: the weak will say to the haughty, 'We were your followers, so can you now relieve us from some share of the Fire?' but they will say, 'We are all in this together. God has judged between his creatures.* xciv

This scene is repeated earlier in the Qur'ān in the chapter Saba, where a group of oppressors and the oppressed who followed them have a similar conversation with a similar result. This is perhaps the most worrying part of the whole notion of living in times of oppression or repression as a Muslim – that my culpability is not offset simply by being from the oppressed, from being a member of the suspect community, there has to be action that offsets my role within the system. For the secret believer, he used his access and his position in order to speak his truth, something that is much harder to do than we might credit. In my world, politicians are so eager to play politics, that somehow the truth has been lost in the process. I often hear of MPs, both Muslim and non-Muslim speak of how they understand that the Muslim community is unfairly targeted, but that it is not politically expedient for them to make those points. It is precisely this form of politicking that I find so utterly objectionable and contemptible – for the first casualty of these conflicts, is always the truth. On occasion, this is manufactured, where 'noble lies' are considered to be a normal part of neo-conservative thinking:

> *The neoconservative have learned a great deal from Leo Strauss's postmodern conception of 'noble lies'. And it must be admitted that postmodernity has removed the stigma that was once associated with lying. In the absence of any reality or absence of power, the creative art rules supreme. In such a world, truth is a construction. Lying is simply creativity. Politics is no longer the domain of judicious lying, or lying to the enemy to ensure survival or avert annihilation. Lying has become synonymous with politics, and politics has become ubiquitous.[xcv]*

The secret believer was from the ruling elite family of Pharaoh. He wasn't an outsider to the system. He wasn't a member of the oppressed population or from their gene pool, but he chose to believe and speak the truth. This is in sharp contrast to the other fringe cousin figure in the Qur'ān, that of Korah, the cousin of Moses, and thus from the Children of Israel. In one place in the Qur'ān, Korah is described as having betrayed the Children of Israel, but perhaps the clearest example of his own complicity against his people is the moment he is included in the group who say, "Kill the sons of those who believe with him [Moses]." [40:23] Korah is clearly included in this group, not as a witness, not as a bystander, but as an active participant in the despotism against his own people – he is the archetypal collaborator as he abandons the truth and his own people for the sake of wealth, prestige and power. In that sense, Korah reminds me of the colonised man described by Franz Fanon in 'Black Skins White Masks':

> *The colonized is elevated above his jungle status in proportion to his adoption of the mother*

country's cultural standards.[xcvi]

Except Korah, as a member of the targeted and disenfranchised community of the Children of Israel has not just adopted the cultural standards of the Pharaonic empire, but has gone further to play a role in the harm against his own community. I wonder: is there anyone in the Qur'ān that is more despicable than this man? As the Qur'ān describes, not all the power or wealth he accumulated was able to save him from his eventual damnation. If you are from the number that make up the oppressed group, you have no option other than to join with those you suffer with, for that is where your ultimate solidarity lies. As I revisit the Jessie Williams speech, he eloquently reminds us of the commodification of the colonised who helps to reinforce oppression:

> *Now the thing is, though, all of us in here getting money - that alone isn't gonna stop this. Alright, now dedicating our lives, dedicating our lives to getting money just to give it right back for someone's brand on our body when we spent centuries praying with brands on our bodies, and now we pray to get paid for brands on our bodies.*

I am increasingly of the view that 'representation' can never be linked to economic or class status, for these are false criteria created by those who seek to maintain hierarchies of authoritarianism. Further, I think it does not take too much thinking, for us to understand that bloodlines are meaningless. Righteousness can never be linked to national identity, blood or genetics. The wife of Pharaoh (who also converted to the religion of Moses) and the secret believer are examples of individuals who spoke truth to power, despite the repercussions that they might face - unlike Korah, who was willing to sell his community for the sake of self preservation and an easy life.

What the two men in the chapter al-Ghafir teach me, is that ethical representation is predicated on the ability to speak the truth of the oppressed, regardless of the community from which you hail. There is little point in pursuing power and authority for the disenfranchised if once an individual is able to scale the heights and hurdles that are placed in the way by the system, they only serve to reinforce the structural racism and discrimination from which they once suffered. In fact, this only serves to reinforce the violence of the state.

While those in authority are important to discuss, ultimately they are not my first concern. My primary interest is how I resist from within my community, and also how I resist with those around me. I feel a sense of tension that many others want to express themselves. They see the discrimination of the state, but they also see how the state can harm and so retreat into pragmatism. I want to think about this carefully because I need to know the points of connection between us. I also need to know if and where there are any boundaries that might separate us.

In that regard, I have always benefitted a great deal from Malcolm X's Michigan State University speech on 23 January 1963 – the famous 'house negro' speech. The speech is so significant in terms of understanding intra-community dynamics, that it is worth reproducing in part:

> *So you have two types of Negro. The old type and the new type. Most of you know the old type. When you read about him in history during slavery he was called "Uncle Tom." He was the house Negro. And during slavery you had two Negroes. You had the house Negro and the field Negro.*

The house Negro usually lived close to his master. He dressed like his master. He wore his master's second-hand clothes. He ate food that his master left on the table. And he lived in his master's house--probably in the basement or the attic--but he still lived in the master's house.

So whenever that house Negro identified himself, he always identified himself in the same sense that his master identified himself. When his master said, "We have good food," the house Negro would say, "Yes, we have plenty of good food." "We" have plenty of good food. When the master said that "we have a fine home here," the house Negro said, "Yes, we have a fine home here." When the master would be sick, the house Negro identified himself so much with his master he'd say, "What's the matter boss, we sick?" His master's pain was his pain. And it hurt him more for his master to be sick than for him to be sick himself. When the house started burning down, that type of Negro would fight harder to put the master's house out than the master himself would.

But then you had another Negro out in the field. The house Negro was in the minority. The masses--the field Negroes were the masses. They were in the majority. When the master got sick, they prayed that he'd die. [Laughter] If his house caught on fire, they'd pray for a wind to come along and fan the breeze.

If someone came to the house Negro and said, "Let's go, let's separate," naturally that Uncle Tom would say, "Go where? What could I do without boss? Where would I live? How would I dress? Who would look out for me?" That's the house Negro. But if you went to the field Negro and said, "Let's go, let's separate," he wouldn't even ask you where or how. He'd say, "Yes, let's go." And that one ended right there.

So now you have a twentieth-century-type of house Negro. A twentieth-century Uncle Tom. He's just as much an Uncle Tom today as Uncle Tom was 100 and 200 years ago. Only he's a modern Uncle Tom. That Uncle Tom wore a handkerchief around his head. This Uncle Tom wears a top hat. He's sharp. He dresses just like you do. He speaks the same phraseology, the same language. He tries to speak it better than you do. He speaks with the same accents, same diction. And when you say, "your army," he says, "our army." He hasn't got anybody to defend him, but anytime you say "we" he says "we." "Our president," "our government," "our Senate," "our congressmen," "our this and our that." And he hasn't even got a seat in that "our" even at the end of the line. So this is the twentieth-century Negro. Whenever you say "you," the personal pronoun in the singular or in the plural, he uses it right along with you. When you say you're in trouble, he says, "Yes, we're in trouble."

But there's another kind of Black man on the scene. If you say you're in trouble, he says, "Yes, you're in trouble." [Laughter] He doesn't identify himself with your plight whatsoever.[xcvii]

Malcolm X was speaking and writing at the height of the black civil rights struggle, when black bodies were routinely detained or killed without reason – but he was largely speaking about this distinction as a metaphor. The late nineteenth century freedman,

Frederick Douglass, wrote one of the most compelling autobiographical accounts of life as a slave, where he described in vivid detail the way in which slaves acclimatised to notions of privilege:

> *It was called by the slaves the Great House Farm. Few privileges were esteemed higher, by the slaves of the out-farms, than that of being selected to do errands at the Great House Farm. It was associated in their minds with greatness. A representative could not be prouder of his election to a seat in the American Congress, than a slave on one of the out-farms would be of his election to do errands at the Great House Farm. They regarded it as evidence of great confidence reposed in them by their overseers; and it was on this account, as well as a constant desire to be out of the field from under the driver's lash, that they esteemed it a high privilege, one worth careful living for. He was called the smartest and most trusty fellow, who had this honor conferred upon him the most frequently. The competitors for this office sought as diligently to please their overseers, as the office-seekers in the political parties seek to please and deceive the people. The same traits of character might be seen in Colonel Lloyd's slaves, as are seen in the slaves of the political parties.[xcviii]*

We have slowly seen a shift towards that time again through the increased killings of black lives in the US by police officers, and through the securitisation of Muslim communities around the world. Malcolm X's analogy still has much relevance, as we seek to understand the relationship between communities and authority – to what extent are we citizens or subjects? Also, to what extent are we personally culpable considering the systemic forms of discrimination that disable us?

The Holocaust remains in its legacy one of the most profound examples of how individuals can be co-opted into carrying out atrocities, even from within oppressed communities. There is an environment that such severe suffering imposes, where all notions of humanity and morality are distorted by the environment. It is Primo Levi's description of the Lager that left me very much unprepared for this reality:

> *They are the typical product of the structure of the German Lager: if one offers a position of privilege to a few individuals in a state of slavery, exacting in exchange the betrayal of a natural solidarity with their comrades, there will certainly be someone who will accept. He will be withdrawn from the common law and will become untouchable; the more power that he is given, the more he will be consequently hateful and hated. When he is given the command of a group of unfortunates, with the right of life or death over them, he will be cruel and tyrannical, because he will understand that if he is not sufficiently so, someone else, judged more suitable, will take over his post. Moreover, his capacity for hatred, unfulfilled in the direction of the oppressors, will double back, beyond all reason, on the oppressed; and he will only be satisfied when he has unloaded onto his underlings the injury received from above.[xcix]*

Writing of the Warsaw Ghetto, Laurence Rees describes how those who were placed in charge of managing the Jews detained within the Ghetto were taken advantage of by some of those put in charge. Abraham Gancwajch is one example of those who used their position in order to undermine and take advantage of his own people. He did this by using thugs would who effectively steal and on occasion rape the local residents, ostensibly through the established December 1940 Office to Combat Usury and Profiteering in the Jewish Quarter of Warsaw. By attacking the religious and cultural life of Jewish people, Gancwajch was able to justify (to himself and his comrades) the horrors they meted out. The experience of the Jews during the Holocaust had a great deal of resonance for others facing the horrors of authoritarianism. Steve Biko recognised their plight during his assessment of the black struggle in Apartheid, specifically acknowledging the role that collaborators played:

> *In Germany the petty officials who decided on which Jews were to be taken away were also Jews. Ultimately Hitler's gangs also came for them. As soon as the dissident factors outside the apartheid institutions are completely silenced, they will come for those who make noise inside the system.*[c]

Despite Levi's dim view of those who collaborate, there are still examples of those who understand that all they can do in their circumstance, is ameliorate conditions as best as possible. In this regard, the story of Adam Czerniaków is one that is pertinent to this discussion on the system and collaborators. His story exemplifies the difficulty of working within an environment where oppression is the daily term of reference, from moving to breathing. I have great sympathy for Czerniaków's position. He was appointed the head of the Warsaw Ghetto Jewish Council – effectively the representative for the Jews in the Ghetto to the Nazis. This is a position that none could or would want, and so it is instructive for us to understand how he acted and the decisions that he made. Adam Czerniaków, a Polish-Jew himself, attempted to manage the affairs of the Ghetto, knowing that if it were not him, it would be someone else. After two years, he was given orders by the SS to provide lists of Jews who would be deported (to their deaths), and he attempted his best to find reasons to exclude large groups from the deportations. When finally the Nazis threatened that it was either to provide lists for deportation or see 100 hostages including his wife killed, Czerniaków chose to commit suicide by swallowing a cyanide capsule. In a note he left before his death, he wrote:

> *They demand me to kill children of my nation with my own hands. I have nothing to do but to die.*[ci]

I cannot begin to imagine the multitude of choices that Adam Czerniaków was forced to make in order to keep the children of his nation safe. When it comes to the notion of 'representation' this is the worst form in which it can come. He was put in a situation where all that he could do, was to try and minimise the harm that could come to his own, and when faced with the prospect of being responsible for the killing of his wife and other hostages, or the alternative, be responsible for the deportation and execution of thousands, it was the kind of catch-22 with which he could not bring himself to be complicit.

For those Jews who survived the horrors of the Holocaust and the concentration camps, their arrival at the Kibbutz communities in Occupied Palestine did little to assuage the anxiety they were feeling. Rather than being greeted as survivors of a horrific trauma, they were blamed for not having taken an active role in their own defence:

> *After the war Auschwitz survivors sometimes*

had to endure taunts that they lacked the courage to resist. Halina Birenbaum remembers that when she reached Israel in 1947 she was distraught when other members of the Kibbutz said to her, "You just followed like sheep you didn't defend yourselves, why didn't you defend yourselves? What happened to you? You're to blame! You didn't do anything. That kind of thing wouldn't happen to us. Don't tell us about it, it's a disgrace. Don't tell the young people, you'll crush their fighting spirit." The history of the Sonderkommando riot at Auschwitz in October 1944 demonstrates the injustice of such accusations. The Sonderkommandos did not go like sheep to the slaughter they fought back and died as a consequence, they lost their lives because effective resistance in Auschwitz was almost impossible. Auschwitz lasted as an institution for four and a half years, and in that time out of the more than 1 million people sent there about 800 attempted to escape but fewer than 150 of them managed to get away from the area, and an unknown number of these successful escapees was subsequently killed in the war. It was then not so much a lack of courage that prevented the inmates escaping as a lack of opportunity.[cii]

The bravado of the Israelis and their mean-spiritedness towards the Holocaust survivors is surprising, considering that it seems that they were aware of what was taking place. Perhaps this will always be the case for those who were not present, that outside of the presence, outside of the ability to directly empathise, a degree of blaming the victim will take place.

The system requires collaborators to rewrite history,

and also to rewrite the future. Part of the strategy of oppression, is to sell the dream of a future world in which one day there will be salvation, and part of that is the salvation of the afterlife. The words of Jesse Williams are pertinent here:

> *Now, freedom is always coming in the hereafter,*
> *but you know what, though, the hereafter is a*
> *hustle. We want it now.*

Jessie Williams's anxiety over the use of the 'hereafter' to symbolise an other worldly emancipation was previously picked up by W.E.B. du Bois, who criticised the quietist strand of activism that a certain reading of Christianity brought. I have the same concerns about quietist readings of Islam, that effectively they are acquiescing of the status quo of injustice, and not only preach patience in the face of injustice but justify the oppression by providing it religious cover. The 'hereafter' is supposed to be a matter of worldly emancipation, giving us confidence in our righteousness, that worldly efforts will have a final justice, but that our effort will be part of the judgement process. In 'The Souls of Black Folk' du Bois wrote:

> *"Children, we all shall be free*
>
> *When the Lord shall appear!"*
>
> *This deep religious fatalism, painted so beautifully in "Uncle Tom," came soon to breed, as all fatalistic faiths will, the sensualist side by side with the martyr. Under the lax moral life of the plantation, where marriage was a farce, laziness a virtue, and property a theft, a religion of resignation and submission degenerated easily, in less strenuous minds, into a philosophy of indulgence and crime. Many of the worst characteristics of the Negro masses of today had*

> *their seed in this period of the slave's ethical*
> *growth. Here it was that the Home was ruined*
> *under the very shadow of the Church, white*
> *and black; here habits of shiftlessness took root,*
> *and sullen hopelessness replaced hopeful strife.*[ciii]

The 'Dreamers' are the ones who permit this sense of acceptance – an acquiescence of the harms that are perpetrated in the hope of something better that is not too distant to reach. In his beautiful epistle to his son, Ta-Nahesi captures so perfectly my own anxieties around the destruction of black and Muslim lives – he intersects them so that we can understand there are pervasive logics that travel from Michael Brown to drone strikes in Yemen. He speaks of the 'Dreamers' – the ones who sell a resolved 'representation' within injustice, and offer the hereafter as a goal in their instruction of pacification:

> *Michael Brown did not die as so many of his*
> *defenders supposed. And still the questions*
> *behind the questions are never asked. Should*
> *assaulting an officer of the state be a capital*
> *offense, rendered without trial, with the officer*
> *as judge and executioner? Is that what we wish*
> *civilization to be? And all the time the*
> *Dreamers are pillaging Ferguson for municipal*
> *governance. And they are torturing Muslims,*
> *and their drones are bombing wedding parties*
> *(by accident!), and the Dreamers are quoting*
> *Martin Luther King and exulting nonviolence*
> *for the weak and the biggest guns for the strong.*
> *Each time a police officer engages us, death,*
> *injury, maiming is possible. It is not enough to*
> *say that this is true of anyone or more true of*
> *criminals. The moment the officers began their*
> *pursuit of Prince Jones, his life was in danger.*
> *The Dreamers accept this as the cost of doing*

> *business, accept our bodies as currency, because*
> *it is their tradition. As slaves we were this*
> *country's first windfall, the down payment on*
> *its freedom.[civ]*

The 'Dreamers' seek 'representation' – they tell me that we need more people of colour police officers, more people of colour politicians, more people of colour judges etc. Yes, we do, because they will add their own value (or not) when they arrive.

Before you tell me that though, I want to know why, after the institutional/structural racism within institutions has been found, that it is impossible to conceive of white police officers as not being racist or discriminatory? Why is representation the panacea when the first question we should be asking is, what stops some white people from being racist in the first place? What if we take that even further, and the brutalised, the ones who are supposed to represent us, become part of the structure of racism that we seek to end? James Forman Jr. captures the extent of this problem perfectly in his incisive analysis of the black contribution to the mass incarceration of black men in America in 'Locking Up Our Own'. Reflecting on the case of his client Brandon, he writes:

> *Brandon and the other young men in the*
> *cellblock who were black. So was everybody in*
> *the courtroom—not just the judge, but the court*
> *reporter, the bailiff, and the juvenile prosecutor.*
> *So was the police officer who had arrested*
> *Brandon, not to mention the police chief and*
> *the mayor. Even the building we were in—the*
> *H. Carl Moultrie Courthouse, named after the*
> *city's first black chief judge—was a reminder of*
> *the African American influence on D.C.'s legal*
> *system.*
>
> *This wasn't my first time in an all-black D.C.*

courtroom, but something—probably my anger at the Martin Luther King speech— made the reality stand out that day. When I got back to my office, I continued the racial tally. I had been to the detention facility that would be Brandon's new home more times than I wanted to count, and I knew that all the guards there were black, too. The city council that wrote the gun and drug laws Brandon had been convicted of violating was majority African American and had been so for more than twenty-five years. In cases that went to trial, the juries were often majority black. Even some of the federal officials involved in D.C.'s criminal justice system were African American, including Eric Holder, then the city's chief prosecutor.

What was going on? How did a majority-black jurisdiction end up incarcerating so many of its own?[cv]

Perhaps, as Forman Jr. recognises, that this is taking place in a majority black jurisdiction, and so it is likely that there will be more black people detained, charged and convicted, but not in the numbers he is seeing. For Forman Jr. the idea of class, and that some black men made it, means that they have to be harder on those who have 'squandered' the privileges that it is perceived they have. Forman Jr.'s evidence takes even further into the way in which racism is internalised, with shocking results:

In 1966, the University of Michigan's Donald Black and Albert Reiss led a team of researchers who rode or walked for weeks with black and white officers in Boston, Chicago, and Washington D.C. What they found was disturbing: though black officers were not as prejudiced as white ones, a significant minority of black officers still expressed antiblack attitudes. The researchers classified 28 percent of the black officers working in black precincts as "highly prejudiced" or "prejudiced." Many of these black officers sounded like Klansmen. One told the researchers, "I'm talking to you as a Negro, and I'm telling you these people are savages. And they're real dirty. We were never rich, but my mother kept us and our home clean." Another said, "There have always been jobs for Negroes, but the f------ people are too stupid to go out and get an education. They all want the easy way out."[xvi]

Representation, in a system that is oppressive, may never be enough. James Forman Jr is not calling those within the system collaborators. He is however asking how short-sighted thinking, that is based on ideas of class, education and privilege, have contributed to a system of mass incarceration that specifically discriminates against black men. Perhaps we can become complicit in our own demise when we don't seek to redress more fundamental/structural issues in the way a system has been constructed?

In that sense, Malcolm X's 'house Negro/field Negro' dichotomy has pertinence at different levels of my thinking. For a start it assumes a relationship between the master and the slave, or the state and the subject, where subjects are at the whim of the state and its excesses. I have some very personal reasons to be interested in this idea, and largely because after the media attempted to vilify me as an individual, particularly the Daily Mail, they presented their frustration by questioning my relationship with the state. The main Daily Mail headline, that still appears as the first Google link to my name said:

A very privileged apologist for evil: An heiress

> *wife. A £700k Surrey home. How the public*
> *school educated 'human rights' champion who*
> *praised Jihadi John lives the good life in the*
> *country he's trying to destroy[cvii]*

This headline came off the back of the Muhammad Emwazi press conference, where I informed the world that the man known as Jihadi John, who the Washington Post claimed was Muhammad Emwazi, had previously been subjected to harassment in the UK by the police and MI5.[cviii] This resulted in a severe backlash by the right-wing and tabloid press, choosing to present me in some kind of opposition to the state. The key paragraph that I want to reflect on in the article says:

> *But, in the eyes of many, both Asim Qureshi and*
> *Cage have questions to answer, not just about*
> *their 'relationship' with Jihadi John, but also*
> *about the poisonous anti-British propaganda*
> *they are spreading against the country that so*
> *welcomed them.[cix]*

Having questions to answer is not a problem, after all, CAGE is asking questions of its own. Our mandate is about full accountability, and in that respect our funding entirely comes from Muslim and non-Muslim communities in the UK with the small exception of some minor grant funding we received for a few years from the Joseph Rowntree Charitable Trust and the Roddick Foundation. Other than that, we have no interests to declare except for our commitment to the Rule of Law, which sits at the heart of all our work. When we advocate on behalf of terrorism suspects, it is on the basis that we do not buy into the state of exception – parity or nothing at all. For the Daily Mail, this is "poisonous anti-British propaganda" because we choose to hold the state to account – we see ourselves as citizens, not subjects. Of course that brings me finally to my actual point, which is that the Daily Mail assumes that I was welcomed to the UK...

I am unsure as to where it is that I should have been welcomed from...

I was born and raised as a South Londoner, and as I discussed earlier about identity, I feel no sense of anxiety over my Britishness, indeed some may say that I am far more British than many at the Daily Mail, except they have the advantage of a white skin that I don't. So what are the markers of this British attitude that the Daily Mail expects from me? I should imagine it has something to being deferential to authority, to say thank you for allowing a dark skinned man to live in these not-so-sunny Isles.

Except that this is not what it means to be British at all. At least that is what I learnt from Locke, Mill, Hobbes, Dickens, Wordsworth, Hardy and the list can go on. Rather, it would seem to me that the Daily Mail is caught somewhere within a Rudyard Kipling fantasy of colonial power, where they have forgotten that the empire no longer exists, except in their minds, and that the new natives are not simply here to serve.

This argument is familiar to me, but not because of myself, but rather because once again the story of Moses and Pharaoh is instructive. Moses, who is adopted by Pharaoh and his wife after being found in a basket, returns to the palace in order to fulfil the mission given to him and his brother Aaron by Allāh:

> *Go, both of you, to Pharaoh and say, 'We bring a message from the Lord of the Worlds: let the Children of Israel leave with us.'*
>
> *Pharaoh said, 'Did we not bring you up as a child among us? Did you not stay with us for many years? And then you committed that crime of yours: you were so ungrateful.* [tr]

Moses has come with a serious message – he is

holding the state to account with only his brother as protection. This takes exceptional bravery, but he chooses to state his case clearly and openly. He is there to end Pharaoh's oppression of his people. The response of Pharaoh is to deflect from the subject matter – he immediately instead tries to remind Moses that the state lavished favours on him, that he was brought up like a son in their house, to make him seem ungrateful for these blessings – he is not a, as we would say today, a citizen – he is a subject of the state's authority like everyone else, and so should know his place. Moses' quick wit however returns them back to the topic at hand, he deflects back to the actual subject matter which is Pharaoh's oppression of the Jews:

> *And is this – that you have enslaved the Children of Israel – the favour with which you reproach me?*[cxi]

Despite the vitriol against me and my family, I take lessons from the story of Moses, that those who cannot bear to engage with the message, will attack the messenger. I also see that when it comes to oppression, then the only loyalty is to the truth, and not safety and security. I think this is the lesson of all our forebears, whether they were the Prophets, or the civil rights leaders this world has been blessed with. The struggle to speak truth to oppression has the same function, but also suffers from the same responses.

What of Malcolm X's 'House Negro' then? Who is he or she and how do they manifest themselves? When they do, how are we to respond to their approaches in normalising the system so that our critique is not only divided, but subject to their 'representation' due to the primary access they are given? In the chapter on the modalities of oppression, I wrote of the way in which divide and rule as a tool, is as old as man himself – at least in the Muslim telling of the story. This action is magnified within the suspect community itself through the use of inducements and privileges. The 'House Negro' is able to take advantage to individually benefit in an environment that the other members of the same oppressed minority are not able to – such as the examples of Korah and those who collaborated with the Nazis.

Written in 1553, Etienne de la Boetie was thinking of this very question on the relationship between authoritarianism and those who are subjects. His damning tract, 'The Politics of Obedience: The Discourse of Voluntary Servitude' railed against those who simply accepted despotism as being the natural order of human existence. He accurately described the function of the state as it harms communities, but also the mechanisms by which it achieves this:

> *Thus the despot subdues his subjects, some of them by means of others, and thus is he protected by those from whom, if they were decent men, he would have to guard himself; just as, in order to split wood, one has to use a wedge of the wood itself. Such are his archers, his guards, his halberdiers; not that they themselves do not suffer occasionally at his hands, but this riffraff, abandoned alike by God and man, can be led to endure evil if permitted to commit it, not against him who exploits them, but against those who like themselves submit, but are helpless.*[cxii]

I recalled it was in Sayyid Qutb's 'In the Shade of the Qur'ān ' that a similar view of the relationship between power and people was expressed, particularly through the lens of Pharaonic power:

> *Pharaoh's declaration [of being 'the' Lord] betrays the fact that he was deceived by his people's ignorance and their submission to his*

authority. Nothing deceives tyrants more than the ignorance and abject submission of the masses. A tyrant is in fact an individual who has no real power or authority. The ignorant and the submissive simply bend their backs for him to ride, stretch out their necks for him to harness with reins, hang down their heads to give him a chance to show his conceit, and forego their rights to be respected and honoured. In this way they allow themselves to be tyrannized. The masses do all this because they are deceived and afraid at the same time. Their fear has no real basis except in their imagination. The tyrant, an individual, can never be stronger than thousands or millions, should they attach proper value to their humanity, dignity, self-respect and freedom.[cxiii]

Although de la Boetie and Qutb identify the relationship between authority and the oppressed well, I also think that they are both harsh in their criticism of the masses – de la Boetie in particular railing against them for their cowardice in other passages. As in the discussions on the Holocaust, the structural nature of the oppression and the fear that it induces can be completely overwhelming, which is why it is so important to understand the nature of power, to demystify it and to make it lose its faux-omnipotence.

The world around me is a distraction, and it is in the distraction that those in power are able to maintain their power – focus on something else! Don't worry about the state of affairs, because the weekend is coming and you can enjoy yourself! I find it hard to enjoy myself though. Even when I relax with my wife and children, I find residual guilt lingering afterwards, for I cannot simply place in a box the stories of those tortured and abused souls whose stories I carry inside my head and whose pain is in my heart. I don't want to be distracted, for then I will lose sight of what is truly important. Etienne de la Boetie provides a useful example of this from the reign of Cyrus The Great, who had invaded in the Lydians and taken their chief city of Sardis:

> *When news was brought to him that the people of Sardis had rebelled, it would have been easy for him to reduce them by force; but being unwilling either to sack such a fine city or to maintain an army there to police it, he thought of an unusual expedient for reducing it. He established in it brothels, taverns, and public games, and issued the proclamation that the inhabitants were to enjoy them. He found this type of garrison so effective that he never again had to draw the sword against the Lydians. These wretched people enjoyed themselves inventing all kinds of games, so that the Latins have derived the word from them, and what we call pastimes they call ludi, as if they meant to say Lydi.*[cxiv]

Distractions are not just in games, they are also in wealth and power. As a conception, Korah has re-emerged again and again in an act of necromancy, his legacy of undermining his own community in order to better his or her position within an authoritarian structure the sought after goal of their compliance. The comedian Trevor Noah has a sketch around the British starting the Commonwealth games as a means of distraction from its crimes globally:

> *That was colonisation done right. That is what I really enjoy, the British done it perfectly... yeah...because now we're friends. We all speak the same languages. We even have a games where we participate together. The*

Commonwealth Games...ironically named. There was nothing common about it. The wealth was in one place. 'Right! Let's forget everything that happened and let's play some games together. You guys have horses where you come from?' 'No we don't' 'Yeah right, we're going to dance horses together, let's do dancing horses.'

'Jamaica, are you going to be joining in?'

'Nah, we're never gonna join in. Ya people never gonna admit what you did to us. We're not gonna play your games. Give us back our sugar, give us back our cane and give us back our gold.'

'Well we can't do that, that's ridiculous, but come and run with us.'

'Will you give us back the gold?'

'No we won't. But we'll let you win it back one medal at a time.'[xxv]

Unsuspecting mendicants were pursued and persuaded by the British Empire (through the East India Company) in its colonial territories to have control wrested from them and placed in the hands of the British. This is perhaps best exemplified by the history of Mir Jafar Ali Khan Bahadur, who became the Nawab of Bengal in 1757 after assisting the British to defeat the previous Nawab, Siraj ud-Daulah. Mir Jafar is remembered in the Indian continent as the ultimate manifestation of collaboration and remembered by India/Pakistan's most celebrated poet Allama Iqbal, who wrote:

> *Jafar (Mir) of Bengal and Sadiq (Mir) of Deccan are a disgrace to the faith, a disgrace to nation, a disgrace to country.[xxvi]*

The Indian parliamentarian and bestselling author Shashi Tharoor has highlighted how the British with so very little, were able to gain the acquiescence of large populations in his book 'Inglorious Empire', and the devastating consequences that arose from this large scale complicity – the very thing that de la Boetie was warning against 300 years previously:

> *It was an extraordinary combination of racial self-assurance, superior military technology, the mystique of modernity and the trappings of enlightenment progressivism—as well as, it must be said clearly, the cravenness, cupidity, opportunism and lack of organized resistance on the part of the vanquished—that sustained the Empire, along with the judicious application of brute force when necessary. The British in India were never more than 0.05 per cent of the population. The Empire, in Hobsbawm's evocative words, was 'so easily won, so narrowly based, so absurdly easily ruled thanks to the devotion of a few and the passivity of the many.[cxvii]*

It is lamentable to imagine that the British empire project was so efficient in its capture and management of India in particular. The British did not just make arrangements in relation to trade and 'protection', but further reorganised life in the colonies to suit a British management system, to the extent that not even religion was left out of their purview. According to Pankaj Mishra, these policies led to a continued 'invisible suffering'.[cxviii] In an original piece of research conducted by Dr Iza R Hussin at Cambridge University, she explains how interaction with colonial authorities changed religion, but also brought it new elitisms among religious structures:

> *In Malaya, the Pangkor Engagement installed a*

British Resident in the state of Perak, the model for indirect rule in the Malay states from 1874. The crucial contribution of these treaties and proclamations to the states that came to be built over them was a new space in their politics—a discrete space for religion and culture, for an "Islamic law" separate from the rest of the state. This new, and newly privileged, space became an arena for the making of new local elite hierarchies, new claims upon and against the state, and new visions of the relationship between Islam and the state.[cxix]

These new scholarly elites led to debates between communities, as one sought to undermine the other through the notion of the true Islamic 'representation'. Hundreds of year old theological fault lines found an arbiter who could provide laws that would permit the immobilisation of the opposing sides. Those who collaborated with the British were considered in different lights, depending on the position of their particular group. One such example is Sir Sayyid of the Aligarh College, who bore the brunt of a great deal of criticism from other religious outfits due to perceptions that he was in bed with the Raj for self-interested reasons. According to the famous Indian poet Akbar Illahabadi:

Give up your literature, say I; forget your history

Break all your ties with shaykh and mosque - it could not matter less.

Go off to school. Life's short. Best not worry overmuch.

Eat English bread, and push your pen, and swell with happiness.

What our respected Sayyid says is good.

Akbar agrees that it is sound and fair.

But most of those who head this modern school

Neither believe in God, nor yet in prayer.

They say they do, but it is plain to see

What they believe in is the powers that be.[cxx]

The legal and administrative fault lines that were created by the British had ramifications that resonated throughout history until the modern world.

But what does Islam itself say about the role of the scholar with the state? This question isn't just academic, it has been central to both resistance and pacification and one that has possibly troubled me more than any other. It can be said, almost without doubt, that the vast majority of Islam's history has seen a judicial class that has largely been under the authority of the subsequent kingships, sultanates, khedival structures or whatever you may wish to call it, for most of them called themselves Caliph, justly or unjustly.

While Etienne de la Boetie was writing of tyranny and politics of obedience in Europe, within the Islamic world, the Sufi scholar 'Abd al-Wahhāb ibn Ahmad ibn 'Alī al-Sha'rānī was considering the exact same questions in his book entitled 'Advice for Callow Jurists and Gullible Mendicants on Befriending Emirs'. A work of both religious and political significance, al-Sha'rānī considered the relationship more specifically between scholarship and power. Drawing on the work of his own teachers, in particular Sayyidī 'Alī al-Khawwās, he provides cogent advice on the ethics of these relationships, and how scholars can safeguard their own spirituality when dealing with those who may fall into tyranny and despotism. Throughout the advice, al-Sha'rānī is very clear on one theme in particular: the scholar should not be materialistically attached to the safety of him or herself and the fineries of the world, while also being close to an emir/caliph/sultan:

> *'Umar ibn 'Abd al-'Azīz said was: "Do not befriend any tyrannical emir with the intention of rebuking him as long as you love this world. Tyrannical emirs cannot be counted on to accept being rebuked. It is better for you to avoid befriending them. Let that be the end of the matter."*[cxxi]

The role of the scholar then is to be beyond reproach, for the law not just to be done, but must be seen to be done, as the English legal maxim describes. The notion of the scholars altruism towards the umma or at least the community that is under the rule of the emir is further highlighted by the fact that he quotes the scholar only being commanded to speak out against tyranny or despotism when directed at others, not when it is directed at the scholar him or herself.[cxxii] In al-Sha'rānī's world, this is not just theory, but it is something he came to practice with those he became close to.

There is a remarkable relationship here, one in which al-Sha'rānī is comfortable with befriending the emir, but is not so under his control that he is not able to call out wrongdoing when he sees it. In the world I live in today, perhaps we have lost this quality from our scholarship. There is not this degree of accountability, albeit it may be taking place privately:

> *I often tell my emir: "Taste the bitterness of the harm you previously caused your enemy—how long you mistreated him and made his life unpleasant so you could take his office, or try to take it, without justification. Take what you deserve for your actions and don't ask me to help you prevent the punishment your enemy*

inflicts on you, making me smell of injustice and wrong, or to entreat Exalted God to turn his heart from hatred of you to love, for this is a most difficult task."[xxxiii]

There is something to admire about al-Sha'rānī as a scholar who is putting forward an ethical stance for scholarly relations with power, but with a keen sense of understanding of how human beings behave. He provides an excellent narrative about the width and breadth of how the scholar or mendicant should interact with authority in terms of moral or spiritual obligations, but then does provide some worldly insights to counter-balance the strength of his assertions:

I heard Sayyidī 'Alī al-Khawwās, may God have mercy on him, say: "The mendicant must learn to be tactful if he befriends an emir and intercedes with him for the victims of wrongdoing. He must not begin by accusing him of wrongdoing on the basis of his first impression, saying to him, 'You are forbidden to do this and thereby you sin, you who have little fear of God,' etc. Instead, he should blame the emir's followers for the wrongdoing and consider it an opportunity for him to do a good deed by interceding with his followers for that victim."

Al-Sha'rānī's tract shows that when we consider the relationship between Islamic scholar or mendicants with the state, then independence should be the primary aspect of that relationship – the scholar must exert as best he can the ability to maintain a form of independence in order to be able to correct the one in authority. This does not mean that the scholar necessarily needs to become an activist and call for outright rebellion against the state, but he should place himself in the position where he is able to speak the truth in a way that takes into account the environment in which he lives. Of course, this will change according to circumstances, but the aspect of truth-speaking must be present.

The idea of the nation-state was and is still traumatic to the Muslim world. As discussed with the umma as a concept, the nation-state came to redefine some of the boundaries that existed, politically, legally, cultural and religiously. For the first time Muslims had to think carefully about where their allegiance lay beyond a general amorphous allegiance to the Caliph and to their own local emirs. These tensions have never been successfully resolved, and due to that, the period of colonisation and post-colonialism has led to tensions between the state and Muslims.

At its most simple level, the tension can be described through positing a scenario: I am a Muslim in Pakistan standing at the border of Afghanistan. I see a man in Afghanistan 1 metre away from me being harmed unjustly, what does Islam say is my obligation in this moment? What do the scholars say is the concept of duty in this circumstance? This is a very simplistic question, but one that draws in the entire history of colonial impact and the redrawing of the borders of the Muslim world since the Sykes-Picot agreement.

Disquiet in the Muslim world has not been specifically connected to the notion of a desire to see a return of the Caliphate, but actually finds its logic in more human needs, the basic rights of dignity and justice – ones that the history of despotism in the region denied them. This was seemingly supposed to carry on in perpetuity - that is, until the Arab Spring. This was the moment that the people - and I will admit to having been carried away with them in their wave - would truly try and reach some semblance of self determination. Muslims en masse celebrated the gains that were coming, and in the process looked to their scholarship to affirm that the umma was still alive. The disappointment that was to come from the religious class, however, is best summarised by Dr Ovamir Anjum, who writes:

> *The courageous and largely peaceful protests against the atrocious injustice and corruption of the ruling elite drew sympathy and admiration from even the most skeptical observers in the world. Yet, the negative response by the traditional Muslim scholarly elite, from the Grand Mufti of Egypt, Shaykh 'Ali Jum'a (Ali Gomaa), to the Syrian traditionalist icon, Shaykh Muhammad Sa'id Ramadan al-Bu'ti and others to such protests, and at times even their support of the autocrats even in their last moments, has once again brought out the question that has puzzled Muslim thinkers and activists for more than a century of attempts at reform and nation building. On the one hand, a large number of Muslims continue to revere Islamic tradition and its authorities, the ulama. Yet, on the other hand, the same Muslim scholarly tradition seems to be out of touch with or utterly deny the need for political justice that the same Muslims so widely and desperately seek. No doubt, prominent ulama have long stood by, and at times even led such protest movements, and Islamic tradition has always possessed strands that reflect such concerns and have come to greater prominence in modern times. But it is difficult to deny the presence of arguably the predominant strand in Islamic scholarship since the onset of the classical period that has been characterized as quietist, apolitical, and compromising (in theory, not*

necessarily in personal conduct) toward usurpers of power.[cxxiv]

In the past, pejorative comments such as 'scholars for dollars' were used against those who attached themselves to the state too closely. This term is however problematic, as it calls into question too deeply the various motivations those scholars have and establishes a dehumanising narrative that is difficult to change. You cannot find the human so easily once you have dehumanised them.

The scholars within Islam are supposed to be our guides, but they are not beyond reproach, as Islam does not grant scholarship infallibility. Yet there remains a strong tension that I cannot see past, that prominent Sunni clerics such as the late Ramadan al-Bu'ti provided spiritual cover to the excesses of the Assad regime. As mentioned by Dr Anjum, it also saw the grand institution of al-Azhar provide religious justification for state sponsored violence against protestors. This theme was picked up by David H Warren, in his assessment of the religious justifications that emanated from Ali Jum'a, during the usurping military regime in Egypt:

> *He [Ali Jum'a] legitimated the coup by drawing on a premodern principle whereby the legitimacy to rule was rooted first and foremost in the capacity to govern effectively (taghallub). The underlying assumption of taghallub is that usurpers' ability to overthrow a ruler demonstrates their de facto ability to ensure stable rule, and therefore their legitimacy. After the coup, Jum'a also gave lectures to the army. In these lectures, Jum'a called the anticoup protesters "rebels" (khawarij) and the "dogs of hell" (kilab al-nar). These terms, originating in Prophetic hadith and the history of early Islam,*

> *appeared to suggest that Jum'a was*
> *legitimating the army's killing of the protestors*
> *on the grounds that they had engaged in*
> *illegitimate rebellion and were no longer*
> *Muslims.*[cxxv]

My question from this line of thinking emerges: how is it then that these institutions and figures can still be considered independent of politics?

The relationship between official institutions and the state have always resulted in difficulty. Even in a post-colonial environment, the centralisation of new politics away from colonial structures resulted in the same process of state sanctioned religion. In her account of the repression of the Muslim Brotherhood during the government of Gamal Abdel Nasir, the prominent women's activist Zainab al-Ghazali, wrote of the official al-Azhar magazine:

> *Even al-Azhar magazine, which was once dear*
> *to our hearts, opened its pages to hypocritical*
> *writers who competed to please falsehood and*
> *its folk. Fatwas which defamed the Mujahids*
> *who opted for 'azimah and shunned the error*
> *they called rukhsah, Began pouring from some*
> *government-employed scholars. They hurled*
> *abuse at those Mujahids who called people to*
> *practise Islam and not merely belong to it by*
> *name; for Islam is practise, not lip service.*[cxxvi]

Rather than being an exception to the rule, this relationship between the official centres of Islamic learning and the state became the norm across the Middle East, resulting in a political ossification despite claims of independence and authenticity.

US President Donald J Trump's visit to Saudi Arabia and participation in an Islamic Summit in the Kingdom is perhaps the latest example of the gross hypocrisy that plagues the Arab and Muslim world.

There is one picture that I cannot erase from my mind: the image of King Salman in the centre, to the right Donald Trump and to the left Abdel Fattah el-Sisi (the usurper President of Egypt). Behind them, fading into shadow, are the other leaders of Muslim countries around the world. As a symbol of how despotism works and the way in which it is propped up by the West, there was literally no more fitting image.

In what can only be described as irony, the purpose of this gathering was to pledge and launch an international centre with the focus on countering violent extremism. Yet, that one picture captured the structural violence of the Muslim world, the structural power that has consistently undermined any form of just rule emerging, for any notion of self determination or equality. Key to that image, is Trump's figure, as the ever present partner on the barrier to Muslim political ambitions.

By working with dictatorships in the Middle East in their counter-terrorism efforts, the US has reminded us that it has no intention to promote democracy as a panacea to strife in the world. Rather the emphasis is on neo-liberalism, whether that is enforced through a democracy or a theocracy. In order to perpetuate that, all that risks it must be demobilised, and through Countering Violent Extremism (CVE), they have a platform to neutralise all political opposition.

The UK is very much seen as the father of CVE work, through the Prevent strategy, which as discussed earlier has a statutory enforcement in place. Prevent is part of the overall counter-terrorism policy in the UK, and is used within that framework to reinforce what the government refers to as soft approaches in counter-terrorism. My organisation CAGE has consistently argued that there is no such thing as a soft approach, when the entire apparatus works interdependently, so where 'voluntary compliance' with Prevent is not obtained, there are other laws that permit sanction or coercion. According to Dr Francesco Ragazzi this interdependence largely functions to demobilise communities, so that they are not able to resist the box of the suspect community:

> *counter-terrorism and counter-terrorism work predominantly as factor of political de-mobilisation. The confusion between community cohesion and counter-terrorist objectives of the Prevent policies has generated a critique of the empowered 'trusted Muslim' depicted as unelected, conservative, unrepresentative community leaders.*[cxxvii]

As Ragazzi rightly points out, that due to the need for Prevent to be, in many ways, self-enforcing, a community based repression sets in. Prevent echoes de la Boetie, who saw that the most effective way to police a community, would be to use members of that community themselves to do the policing. Of course, for Muslims, this sets up the 'good Muslim bad Muslim' narrative, as those who comply with the government's aims and objectives are seen as compliant, whereas those who do not are seen as rebellious or subversive. It is in fact the worst form of social-engineering, as it lends itself to friction within the community. In 'The Muslims are Coming', Arun Kundnani eloquently describes how the Prevent programme lent itself to the colonial logic of the preferred elite:

> *Community leaders who were more interested in building up their own ethnic fiefdoms than in advocating on behalf of the people they claimed to represent could be relied on to parrot the official line, terrorism was caused by the virus of extremism and best eradicated with an injection of British values. Prevent created a mini-industry of groups and organizations willing to*

give the government's message a Muslim face. Those who took a different view—for example, on questions of foreign policy—were put under pressure. On the eve of the publication of a new version of the Prevent strategy in March 2009, the government wrote a letter to the Muslim Council of Britain, the most prominent national Muslim organization, stating that unless its then deputy general secretary, Daud Abdullah, resigned, it would sever relations with the organization.[cxxviii]

Part of the problem with the Prevent aspect of counter-terrorism policy, is that its logic is too tied to the idea that threats exists in an exceptionality, and so that it must try and attempt to predict future harm. The problem that comes with this, is that when the legal system becomes so wide, and the numbers of detentions due to non-violent offences increase, you begin to run out of suspects. Thus the previously evidence-based criminal justice system is injected with uncertainty born from the intrinsically speculative nature of intelligence. In the main it is not tested in open court and that the probability of doing so is further diminished by new closed material procedures that conspire to limit the extent to which open justice operates. Reliance on such "intelligence" lowers the bar for sanction and makes the courts vulnerable to politicisation. It also enables the targeting of whole communities as nascent threats.

This is nothing new, in the context of Latin America in the late 1960s, President Nixon became particularly worried by the emergence of Catholic liberation theology and its revolutionary nature in seeking redress for oppressed people. This was followed up even into the Regan administration, who used research conducted by the Rand Corporation to establish the

Institute of Religion and Democracy (IRD), a body specifically established to counteract liberation theology, primarily through incorporating Catholic priests themselves.[cxxix]

On the merry-go-round, individuals take their turn until they come to a spotlight, where they are found and removed, only for the 'next' most dangerous individual or group to be identified. All the while the government keeps close to it those who will never waiver from the accepted narrative, and they are put forward to constantly remind communities that the government does engage and listen to Muslims – except that those Muslims they listen to financially and socially benefit from the relationships:

> *The Quilliam Foundation received over £1 million of government Prevent funding in its first two years. But things came unstuck in late 2009 after Ed Husain gave an interview to the Guardian in which he acknowledged Prevent was "gathering intelligence on people not committing terrorist offences" and said that to do so was "good" and "right." This proved somewhat embarrassing at a time when ministers were trying to reassure the public that Prevent did not involve intelligence gathering but was a form of community engagement and assistance. The government was forced to distance itself from the foundation. The following year, Husain and Nawaz hoped they might return to favor with the new Conservative-led coalition government that came to power in May 2010.[cxxx]*

It is now largely accepted within the world of terrorism experts who have studied the issue for many years, that this politics of 'good Muslim bad Muslim' will never achieve its stated goals, as those who put forward as the acceptable arbiters, will invariably be rejected by communities. Those relationships, based on power, economic interest and coercion are frail. They cannot stand the test of time.

The Nazis were never the friends of the Jews they put in control of the Warsaw Ghetto, any more than Senator McCarthy was a friend to Jackie Robinson. These were vertical relationships that were based around environments of fear and coercion, and thus their frailty lay within their cruelty – a notion beautifully captured by Etienne de la Boetie:

> *The fact is that the tyrant is never truly loved, nor does he love. Friendship is a sacred word, a holy thing; it is never developed except between persons of character, and never takes root except through mutual respect; it flourishes not so much by kindnesses as by sincerity. What makes one friend sure of another is the knowledge of his integrity: as guarantees he has his friend's fine nature, his honor, and his constancy. There can be no friendship where there is cruelty, where there is disloyalty, where there is injustice. And in places where the wicked gather there is conspiracy only, not companionship: these have no affection for one another; fear alone holds them together; they are not friends, they are merely accomplices.*[cxxxi]

We need to think better about what we actually know about violence and movements, cultures and subcultures, in order to better think about how we can engage power both internally and externally. We need to think more about the epistemological approaches we take to violence, and so we must turn to experts who help us to move past the last sixteen years of failed policy in the War on Terror.

Acceptance within society cannot be achieved

through parachuting outsiders to the community in as the solution. They need a record of organising, activity and independence that makes them immune to the criticism that they are compromised. Communities need to have seen the product to permit individuals or groups to speak on their behalf. This is the only real truth of 'representation', it can only be real if it has independence, pedigree and truth – without these qualities, any claim to 'representation' will be flatly rejected by those who have been in the trenches:

> *And let's get a couple things straight, just a little sidenote - the burden of the brutalized is not to comfort the bystander. That's not our job, alright - stop with all that. If you have a critique for the resistance, for our resistance, then you better have an established record of critique of our oppression. If you have no interest, if you have no interest in equal rights for black people then do not make suggestions to those who do. Sit down.[cxxxii]*

A Virtue of Disobedience

A Virtue Of Disobedience

"If you cultivate something volatile, you are playing with fire."
[Lemony Snicket - The Grimy Grotto]

"There are times when the world is rearranging itself, and at times like that, the right words can change the world."
[Orson Scott Card - Ender's Game]

"I want to tell the rebels that I am alive. That I'm right here in District Eight, where the Capitol has just bombed a hospital full of unarmed men, women, and children. There will be no survivors." The shock I've been feeling begins to give way to fury. "I want to tell people that if you think for one second the Capitol will treat us fairly if there's a cease-fire, you're deluding yourself. Because you know who they are and what they do." My hands go out automatically, as if to indicate the whole horror around me. "This is what they do! And we must fight back!"
I'm moving in toward the camera now, carried forward by my rage. "President Snow says he's sending us a message? Well, I have one for him. You can torture us and bomb us and burn our districts to the ground, but do you see that?" One of the cameras follows as I point to the planes burning on the roof of the warehouse across from us. The Capitol seal on a wing glows clearly through the flames. "Fire is catching!" I am shouting now, determined that he will not miss a word. "And if we burn, you burn with us!"
[Suzanne Collins - Mockingjay]

A Virtue Of Disobedience

Throughout the pages of this book, I have done my best to understand the world that I see before me through the lens of my religion and my politics. I have always considered my faith to be emancipatory and fresh, one that is able to confront the problems of the world with mercy and justice. But what would my virtue of disobedience look like more formally. Where does this disobedience find its ethic and its power? I want to find the source of our resistance, so that it does not just become a strategy, but becomes part of the way that we live our lives and becomes part of the way in which we find faith.

This virtue of disobedience must be located in three sites of resistance:
1. Language
2. Knowledge
3. Community

I have chosen to concentrate on these areas in particular, because through language we identify ourselves, or perhaps more worryingly, are identified. Knowledge is crucial, for without it, we are subject to the whims of those who occupy the realm of fiction – facts and science can form as part of effective resistance. Finally, and potentially the strongest aspect of any effective resistance, must be unity of resistance through solidarity among the disenfranchised. This is not simply restricted to the community itself, but it is about reversing the divisions that allow for us to be oppressed by the actions of those in authority.

By understanding these three areas, and the ways in which they intersect with resistance, what I hope will emerge is a virtue of disobedience to tyranny. If this can contribute to the discourse around Muslim civic engagement, then God willing, my purpose of writing this book will have been achieved.

This conversations must be opened up. The state of exception and despotism cannot be accepted, and

Islamic scholars cannot simply say that our time will come in the hereafter alone. I am with Jessie Williams: the hereafter is a hustle sold by quietists who do not have the imagination to dream of a world that is free – I reject the pessimism of the quietists.

My community is still reeling from the attack. It happened the same night that news of the rape and murder of Nabra Hassanen in Virginia, US was circulating across social media. In the early hours of Monday 21 June 2017, I began receiving messages from friends in the local area that a van had ploughed straight into a group of Muslims who were leaving from their night-time Ramadan payers. Darren Osborne, a Cardiff resident, drove his van into these Muslims seemingly to attack them.

Darren Osborne was subdued by the congregants of the mosque, and protected from reprisal attacks by the Imam, who ensured that he was kept safe until the police arrived. Four days later, as I write this, we find that a post-mortem determined that 51-year-old Makram Ali died as a result of multiple injuries.

This is not the only attack to have taken place against Muslims. There are thousands of hate crimes that take place yearly, with perhaps the last significant attack being carried out by Pavlo Lapshyn, who killed Birmingham resident Mohammad Saleem. As we know from a 2015 YouGov poll, negative perceptions of Muslims in the UK are only secondary to Roma/Gypsies, and stands at around 40% of the country. Mistrust of police within communities historically since the 1980s has resulted in individuals often not coming forward with their stories of abuse. Three weeks ago, the daughter of a friend was punched in the face twice after the London Bridge attacks. The list goes on – mostly with Muslim women being targeted.

On BBC Newsnight on 19 June 2017, Evan Davis

entered into a discussion with journalist and political commentator Nesrine Malik about the grievances that are felt after the Finsbury Park attack. The exchange is worth producing because of what it tells us:

> [NM] *Whenever there is an attack by a Muslim, people feel that there is a perception of the way the media portrays it as a very coordinated coherent culpability on behalf of all Muslims. And then the perpetrator...*

> [ED] *Well that's not fair. No one says it's all Muslims. Everyone is always careful to make sure that no one is...*

> [NM] *No no no...I'm not saying that everyone does that, but I'm saying there is a perception that that happens. Certain types of words are used, certain language is used. People ask questions like, what is the Muslim community's response to this? So people generally get the impression that there is a generalised culpability. That impression is also reinforced when the attacker is not Muslim. The language is kind of around the fact that he is a misfit or that he is vulnerable. We've heard that around the Jo Cox murder, there's lots of right-wing tabloids that portrayed him as someone who had fears of losing his council house...*

> [ED] *Trying to explain it away...which might be the right thing to do, but then do it for both sides.*

Nesrine Malik does an excellent job of dissecting the way in which 'white' violent crime is problematised through language, as opposed to violence perpetrated by Muslims. What is more crucial, however, is that Evan Davis is very quick to cut Malik off before she can make her point. He says that 'everyone is careful', but who does he mean by everyone? This is not the feeling on the ground within Muslim communities, who read the same newspapers and watch the same media outlets as everyone else. In a thread on his twitter account, Dr Rizwaan Sabir, an academic at the Liverpool John Moores University made similar points, remarking:

> *This is contextualised reporting but it's usually missing when the attacker is non-white; hence surfacing of charges of press hypocrisy.*
>
> *My advice to the press: pls explain possible motivation for 'terrorism' in a nuanced way but pls grant ths privilege to non-white folk too*

Please do not get me wrong. I am not one of those who jumps on the bandwagon of calling for parity of unjust treatment for all, quite the opposite, I feel that we should always bring understanding and mitigation into crimes, to better understand the widest context in which they take place. My own post on Facebook reinforced this point on 19 June 2017 where I decried a double standard that exists when we use a language for other communities that we challenge for ourselves. So if we complain about the use of the word terrorism, then we should not be so quick to turn to the use of the word when someone from the far-right engages in an act of politically motivated violence.

The double standard is important to reflect on, because it is precisely in the language that we use that determines how we treat others. It was interesting to note that during this entire period, there were a number of stories intersecting about Muslims that strayed from the dominant discourse of securitisation, but somehow managed to circle back to it, even if it was implicitly. I saw the Imam of the Muslim Welfare House Mosque in Finsbury Park, who protected his attacker, being praised, but the media describing the other congregants in animalistic terms, as if they were about tear their attacker apart with their teeth – so praise was reserved in the singular – in this Imam who became exceptional, rather than the norm. This evisceration of the Muslims as saviours, was once again present in a series of tweets by the BuzzFeed journalist Aisha Gani, decrying the double standards in relation to the rescue role played by Muslims and mosques after the Grenfell Tower fire:

> *I'm fed up by how wider press mentioned "churches, community centres and temples" and don't care to highlight role of mosques in this*

> *We know how press pack runs to the mosque after a terror attack – the obvious place right – but why is there so little interest in this case*

> *Anyway I am exasperated and never has lack of diversity in press and authorities been so apparent*

I think it is important to listen to the voice of this Muslim woman wearing a hijab who works for one of the most widely read media outlets in the world. Gani's frustration is telling because the narrative around Muslims, and the lack of scientific nature of the discussions around Muslims is significant in terms of perceptions. I can almost hear her scream at her phone as the messages come up, because it is a scream that has issued from my own throat as well as many others I know. Where does her (very understandable) call for representation stand though?

Organisations such as the one I am involved in, CAGE, and like Muslim Engagement & Development (MEND), largely take the view that the problem we face is not solvable through mere 'representation' alone, particularly when that comes from above. As Shenaz Bunglawala writes in 'What is Islamophobia?':

> *A point of reference between the two organisations is concurrence with the view that British Muslims are faced with 'an aggressive anti-Muslim narrative that is based on assumptions [which] subverts the political expression/identity of [Muslim] individuals by turning them into potential threats'.*
>
> *It should be further noted that CAGE and MEND occupy a common status concerning offensive/defensive strategies, with both organisations identified as the main protagonists against 'social movements from above'. The classification of the two organisations as constituting, among others, 'extremist opposition to Prevent' is illustrative of this.* [xxxiii]

It is in our rejection of the status quo, that not only are we seen as threats, but also seen as being traitors to the state. We reject that it is the notion of social movements from above that will result in our ability to find a voice to our politics, to being able to deal with the injustices we see not only perpetrated against our communities, but against others as well.

Language

These entire debates are constructed by the prevailing discourse of the day. The clearest exposition of language as a site of resistance and disobedience to authoritarianism comes in my view from Timothy Snyder, who warns us how language is used to manipulate fears:

> *Listen for dangerous words*
>
> *Be alert to the use of the words extremism and terrorism. Be alive to the fatal notions of*

emergency and exception. Be angry about the
treacherous use of patriotic vocabulary.[cxxxiv]

Had I not more to say, I would have left these words
here as reason enough to make my case that language
must remain for us all a place from which we challenge
authority. In the discussion above, we can see how acts
are treated differently based on the community that is
being examined, and this then becomes a hallmark for
the creation of a suspect community – one that is
exceptionalised. As he does with the rest of his book,
Snyder expands on his ideas, so that they become
teaching tools for those looking to recognise the
repression of the state:

When politicians today invoke terrorism they
are speaking, of course, of an actual danger. But
when they try to train us to surrender freedom
in the name of safety, we should be on our
guard. There is no necessary tradeoff between
the two. Sometimes we do indeed gain by losing
the other, and sometimes not. People who assure
you that you can only gain security at the price
of liberty usually want to deny you both.

Extremism certainly sounds bad, and
governments often try to make it sound worse
by using the word terrorism in the same
sentence. But the word has little meaning.
There is no doctrine called extremism. When
tyrants speak of extremists, they just mean
people who are not in the mainstream—as the
tyrants themselves are defining that
mainstream at that particular moment.[cxxxv]

The vernacular is fixed for us. When the terms
'radical' or 'extremist' are used, it is always to vilify, or
neutralise the opponent. Perhaps, part of our
disobedience could be to turn these terms on their

head, to not permit them to rule us as they seek to rule. In one of my favourite letters, Martin Luther King Jr's 'Letter from a Birmingham Jail' captures this sentiment so perfectly:

> *But though I was initially disappointed at being categorized as an extremist, as I continued to think about the matter I gradually gained a measure of satisfaction from the label. Was not Jesus an extremist for love...Was not Amos an extremist for justice...Was not Martin Luther an extremist...So the question is not whether we will be extremists, but what kind of extremists we will be. Will we be extremists for hate or for love? Will we be extremists for the preservation of injustice or for the extension of justice?[cxxxvi]*

It would be wrong of me in this regard to quote Martin, without quoting Malcolm. Although Martin Luther King Jr was considered to be seditious in his time, both then and later, he was presented as a moderate foil to the more 'extreme' Malcolm X. The famous Oxford Union debate in which Malcolm X engaged, remains for me the best exposition of the use of the term extremism as a juxtaposition to language, and the way that language is used as a means of criminalisation and de-politicisation:

> *I think the only way one can really determine whether or not extremism in defense of liberty is justified, is not to approach it as an American or a European or an African or an Asian, but as a human being. If we look upon it as different types, immediately we begin to think in terms of extremism being good for one and bad for another, or bad for one and good for another. But if we look upon it, if we look upon ourselves as human beings, I doubt that anyone will deny*

that extremism in defense of liberty, the liberty of any human being, is no vice. Anytime anyone is enslaved or in any way deprived of his liberty, that person, as a human being, as far as I'm concerned he is justified to resort to whatever methods necessary to bring about his liberty again.

But most people usually think in terms of extremism as something that's relative, related to someone whom they know or something that they've heard of. I don't think they look upon extremism by itself or all alone. They apply it to something. A good example, and one of the reasons that it can't be too well understood today: many people who have been in positions of power in the past don't realize that the power —centers of power—are changing. When you're in a position of power for a long time, you get used to using your yardstick, and you take it for granted that because you've forced your yardstick upon others, that everyone is still using the same yardstick. So that your definition of extremism usually applies to everyone.

But nowadays times are changing, and the center of power is changing. People in the past who weren't in a position to have a yardstick, or use a yardstick of their own, are using their own yardstick now. And you use one and they use another. In the past, when the oppressor had one stick and the oppressed used that same stick, today the oppressed are sort of shaking the shackles and getting yardsticks of their own. So when they say extremism, they don't mean what you do. And when you say extremism, you don't mean what they do. There's entirely two

> *different meanings. And when this is*
> *understood, I think you can better understand*
> *why those who are using methods of extremism*
> *are being driven to them.*[cxxxvii]

Malcolm X speaks in a way that few others can. He has an ability to unpick a matter and expose it completely so that it is left naked before the world, and little doubt is left as to the strength of his conscience. In that regard, this is where our site of resistance emerges, within language itself.

We cannot continue in an environment where we do not challenge the racist and bigoted vernacular of those who demonise us on a daily basis. Their language reinforces their fears at all levels, the political, the media, the courts and the classroom. By choosing to accept their terms of reference for the debate, we choose to ultimately harm ourselves, for we can never consider ourselves as anything outside of the boxes in which they put us. As Yassir Morsi reflects in 'Radical Skin, Moderate Masks':

> *Act one therefore is when a Muslim accepts the*
> *narrator's call. It is when we accept the role of*
> *telling our story, telling it within the story of*
> *the war on terror; a story-within-a-story; when*
> *we accept its vocabulary, when we remain blind*
> *to its trap. Here, when we speak about*
> *ourselves, when we speak about Islam, 'meaning*
> *is not inside a kernel (of a true us) but outside' of*
> *us and part of the War on Terror's story.*[cxxxviii]

Thus, a Muslim cannot be violent and non-violent – he has to pick a side between the two. As a dissenter to the state, in order to justify my citizenry, I must completely reject the notion of violence, or I am a terrorist or a terrorist sympathiser. But of course, there is one other caveat. I am permitted to believe in violence, as long as it is for the state. In this case, the state provides me carte blanche to justify violent means, to reinforce the imperialism of its military industrial complex.

When the word 'Islamist' is used, we are told that it means those Muslims who believe that Islam is linked to the political, that their faith informs their political life. This is exemplified by David Cameron's Munich speech in 2011 when he said:

> *We need to be absolutely clear on where the origins of these terrorist attacks lie – and that is the existence of an ideology, 'Islamist extremism'. And we should be equally clear what we mean by this term, distinguishing it from Islam. Islam is a religion, observed peacefully and devoutly by over a billion people. Islamist extremism is a political ideology, supported by a minority.*[cxxxix]

Of course, why wouldn't it, faith usually means something all pervading, and yet David Cameron attempts to secularise faith from the world in which it exists. What he really means, however, is that faith should not allow you to think beyond the loyalties owed to the nation state. It means that the only form of politics that are permitted, are ones that structurally reinforce the apparatus of the state, and it cultural hegemony.

The only acceptable form of violence for British citizens, is either for British Jews to go abroad to fight for Israel, for young men and women to become members of private military contractors, or for citizens to join the British army, navy or air force. The ethical boundaries of what is accepted is squarely limited to this arena.

When al-Azhar University in Cairo issues fatwas praising the killing of protestors, providing religious sanction to mass arrest, torture and false imprisonment

– then this is not 'Islamism' – because Islamism is only ever when the interests of the state are threatened, no matter how oppressive that state might be. Thus, we should call this out and say, for authority, 'Islamism' is when dissent is based around religious and spiritual terms, not when the religious is connected to the political. Al-Azhar is clearly political Islam. By extension, it could be said that all state controlled or state affiliated religious institutions are political.

When the Imam for the British Armed Forces, Asim Hafiz, says that what he does is part of his faith and what his faith expects of him, then he is not only making a religious statement, he is also making a political one.[cxl] It is political, because he then intrudes on the territory of providing religious cover to Muslims participating in fighting abroad in conflicts that do not fit with the conscience – let alone fighting against other Muslim countries. Could it be posited that there could be a legitimate intervention that Muslims could participate in? Yes, but that would need to be by the consensus of scholarship in the UK, not the arbitrary political posturing of those in close employ of the British government – perhaps in an instance where the British army finally decided to intervene against the Apartheid regime of Israel. By the definition of 'Islamism' that is applied to UK Muslims, Asim Hafiz is seemingly an Islamist.

Language is a weapon of the state to neutralise. If language is their weapon, then we must turn that weapon on them and call language the first site of resistance towards a virtue of disobedience. We must not permit language to dictate our identity and ethics to us, but rather, we should use language to assert our beliefs, dreams and existence. Language will one day take us through survival, into emancipation, as Primo Levy described:

"Then for the first time we became aware that our language lacks words to express this offence, the demolition of a man. In a moment, with almost prophetic intuition, the reality was revealed to us: we had reached the bottom. It is not possible to sink lower than this; no human condition is more miserable than this, nor could it conceivably be so. Nothing belongs to us any more; they have taken away our clothes, our shoes, even our hair; if we speak, they will not listen to us, and if they listen, they will not understand. They will even take away our name: and if we want to keep it, we will have to find ourselves the strength to do so, to manage somehow so that behind the name, something of us, of us as we were, still remains."[cxli]

Knowledge

Actually, the point is that the Sublime specified that knowledge of evidence is a powerful authority (sultan) because it allows one to have dominance and power over those who are ignorant. Moreover, the power of knowledge is stronger than the might of force as people are more willing to follow evidence than force. In reality, the hearts follow evidence while only the body surrenders to force.

Evidence captivates the heart and guides it. Even if someone is apparently stubborn and arrogant, his heart must surrender to its power and be overcome by it. Moreover, the power of rulers, if not accompanied by knowledge to administer it, is like the power of predatory beasts, lions and the like, i.e. force without knowledge or mercy. Yet the power of

*authoritative evidence is [best exhibited] when
it is accompanied by knowledge, mercy and
wisdom.*

*Finally, if someone is not empowered by
knowledge it is either because his evidence is
weak or because the force used against him is
overwhelming. Otherwise, evidence itself is
necessarily victorious over falsehood.*[cxlii]

These words from the fourteenth century scholar Ibn
al-Qayyim al-Jawziyya provide the perfect basis from
which to consider knowledge itself as one of the sites of
resistance. The very act of knowing something, is in
itself emancipating, for it provides the mind with the
ability to understand circumstances in a way that the
ignorant cannot. What I particularly love about this
statement, is that it redraws truth as one that is based
on evidence not force. These descriptions are
inspirational because at the heart of them is the
recognition that empowerment comes from within: it
comes from a base of knowledge and with that
knowledge the ability to move.

Knowledge, however, can sometimes be a trickster,
even for the well intentioned. Cutie, the robot, cannot
fathom humans having created it in Isaac Asimov's 'I
Robot', leaving the men bewildered, but to
acknowledge:

*"You can prove anything you want by coldly
logical reason---if you pick the proper
postulates."*

Cutie is an honest broker. By no means did it think
for a moment that it would rig its knowledge base to
draw false conclusions – but then Cutie is a robot after
all. It can be forgiven for not having sufficient data to
draw the correct conclusions that were being
demanded of it. The same cannot be said of the world

of securitisation and militarised policing. This is a world that requires (for its existence to be justified) to be in a constant state of threat management. In keeping with taking lessons from 'On Tyranny' by Timothy Snyder, he reminds us of two lessons:

> *Believe in truth.*
>
> *To abandon facts is to abandon freedom. If nothing is true, then no one can criticize power, because there is no basis upon which to do so. If nothing is true, then all is spectacle. The biggest wallet pays for the most blinding lights.*
>
> ...
>
> *Be calm when the unthinkable arrives.*
>
> *Modern tyranny is terror management. When the terrorist attack comes, remember that authoritarians exploit such events in order to consolidate power. The sudden disaster that requires the end of checks and balances, the suspension of freedom of expression, the right to a fair trial, and so on, is the oldest trick in the Hitlerian book. Do not fall for it.*[cxliii]

The adage tells us that truth is the first casualty of war, but it seems that often in the world of securitisation, truth is the first casualty full stop. In June 2015, I wrote a long essay for the online platform Media Diversified, reflecting on the logics that securitised 'gansta rap' music and jihadi songs.[cxliv] The basic premise of my argument was that the songs, whether jihadi or rap, reflect life, rather than create violence of their own. There was a big difference between proving they were causally linked and the fact that there was a multitude of circumstances that correlated certain types of violence to certain emerging popular cultures. It was in the early 1990s that the chief of police for New York made the public case that music can incite violence, and sought to link rap music to the deaths of his officers. The rebuttal was simple enough... if rap music incites violence, why were white people who listened to the same music not killing police officers too? There must have been other intervening factors, such as social deprivation, police brutality and corruption, and other markers that could then go further in explaining – first why that culture existed – and second why officers were targeted.

Often the most basic of maths exercises can help clear the fog of war, especially when basic maths is used in order to make cases. In March 2017, the neo-conservative think tank The Henry Jackson Society released a report, 'Islamist Terrorism: Analysis of Offences and Attacks in the UK (1998-2015)'.[cxlv] The report gained a great deal of press attention over what were presented as startling statistics about the threat that is posed to the UK, stating that the UK was facing a "major home grown threat". Except...their numbers did not add up to that conclusion.

Lowballing the number of British Muslims to be at 2.5 million during that period, out of the 253 terrorism convictions they cited, the vast majority were for non-violent offences, and made up a proportion of 0.01% of the British Muslim population. In real terms, their figures were tantamount to 22 cases over a 17 year period. Even their claim that the number of women involved tripled over recent years, in total put the figure at 18 women over 17 years, and thus 0.001% of the female Muslim population in the UK. My aim here is not to suggest that there is no threat – clearly there is – but the question returns, to what extent do we need the sprawling counter-terrorism legislation that exists for this relatively low percentage threat? To what extent could it in fact make matters worse?

Professor Marc Sageman has, perhaps, produced one

of the most statistically accurate analyses of the terrorism threat in his book 'Misunderstanding Terrorism'. In the book he relies on Bayesian probability to determine the threat levels posed by Muslims living in the West:

> *The first step in calculating this probability is to determine the actual base rate of terrorists in a given population. The survey in the previous chapter listed 66 global neojihadi serious plots or attacks, comprising 220 individuals, directly involving violence in the West in the post-9/11 decade. This amounts to an average of about six and a half serious incidents involving 22 individuals per year. Given a population of about 700 million people in the West, this comes to about three new terrorists per 100 million Westerners per year. However, the perpetrators of this wave of political violence are Muslims and this fact (a new condition for computing this probability) dramatically increases the base rate among Muslims. The Muslim population in the West is unknown, but most estimates put it around 25 million. Thus 22 perpetrators in a population of about 25 million gives a base rate of new terrorists of a bit less than one per million Muslims in the West per year.*[cxlvi]

The statistics are stark and very much speak for themselves. I could go on and quote a great deal more data about how Europol yearly reports on terrorism indicates that Muslim political violence in Europe nearly every year constitutes less than 2% of all violent acts – but then what would be the point? It seems that the debate has shifted far beyond that now. For those who are interested in the subject of terrorism and are not tied to neo-conservative think tanks or married to specific government policies, their view has very much reached the point where they are pushing for a rethink. Experts such as Olivier Roy, Thomas Hegghammer and even I would dare to say Peter Neumann and Shiraz Maher have moved from positions they previously held. In that regard, I think one of the most honest remarks about the state of current counter-terrorism thinking again comes from Professor Sageman:

> *Since both parties of a conflict are responsible for this escalation, one cannot understand the turn to violence without addressing the state's contribution to this outcome. And with the exception of the work of some rare scholars, this state contribution to the emergence of terrorism has been neglected in the literature. Of course, one can attribute this to the fact that states fund most terrorism research, but this cynical interpretation is not the whole story. Honest scholars in the field self-categorize on the side of the state and, like any other in-group member in a conflict, are blind to their own in-group's contribution to the process and completely blame the out-group for any violence. The state contribution to the process leading to political violence may be the most important still unexplored topic in the field. Acknowledgment of this contribution will help us understand this process and may even start a counter process that can defuse this type of political violence before it erupts.*[cxlvii]

How does the state hold up a mirror to itself though? This is the crucial question when the production of actual knowledge is predicated on so many other ideas and interests. Like Plato's cave, the public is shown the dance of the shadows before their eyes, and this is the future fear of terrorist acts, but in reality the puppets are arms deals to Saudi Arabia and the UAE so that they can bomb innocent people in Yemen – whether you are on the divide of neo-conservatism or neo-liberalism, ethics fall away before revenue production. It is precisely in these connections that we need to understand what is taking place behind the scenes – how are Muslim lives constructed from the outside, so that we can resist from the inside?

Prior to the First Gulf War, prior to the first World Trade Centre attack, prior to the East Africa bombings in 1998, there was Bernard Lewis, writing his infamous 1990 essay in The Atlantic entitled 'The Roots of Muslim Rage':

> *"It should by now be clear, that we are facing a mood and a movement far transcending the level of issues and policies and the governments that pursue them. This is no less than a clash of civilizations – the perhaps irrational but surely historical reaction of an ancient rival against our Judeo-Christian heritage, our secular present, and the worldwide expansion of both."*[cxlviii]

For Lewis, any suggestion that there is a history of racism or imperialism has had an impact on the relations between the East and West, is a distraction from the main issue, for he cannot conceive of a Muslim politics outside of his fear of the Qurʾān and Islam as a religion. He further rejects that western backing of despotism in the Middle East has had any bearing on the levels of disenfranchisement – rather, he places the blame squarely at the door of Islam as a culture and Muslims' non-ability to embrace modernity.

In his seminal work 'Orientalism' Edward W Said highlights the contradictions that exist within Lewis's work and his critiques of Islam:

> *Lewis is cavalier with himself and with his*

cause. He will, for example, recite the Arab case against Zionism (using the "in" language of the Arab nationalist) without at the same time mentioning— anywhere, in any of his writings — that there was such a thing as a Zionist invasion and colonization of Palestine despite and in conflict with the native Arab inhabitants. No Israeli would deny this, but Lewis the Orientalist historian simply leaves it out. He will speak of the absence of democracy in the Middle East, except for Israel, without ever mentioning the Emergency Defense Regulations used in Israel to rule the Arabs; nor has he anything to say about "preventive detention" of Arabs in Israel, nor about the dozens of illegal settlements on the militarily occupied West Bank of Gaza, nor about the absence of human rights for Arabs, principal among them the right of immigration, in former Palestine.[cxlix]

Three years later, Samuel Huntington would extend this argument in his own article, describing the 'Clash of Civilisations', for him it is Islam itself that 'has bloody borders'. The extension of the argument is based on the refocusing of Lewis on the religion of Islam itself as the problem, that these are wars, and central to the responses to political violence in our current era, that terrorism is a product of a classical reading of Islam.

These wars of culture, proselytised by Lewis and Huntington, have largely informed American neo-conservatism policy in the US, particularly in matters to do with national security, but in a Jacksonian model of responding. The basic premise is that if America is attacked, then whoever has provoked it must not just be resisted, but completely annihilated in order for the world to receive the message that the US is not open to be attacked in any way.

This is why, on both sides of the Atlantic, we find that think tanks with deeply set neo-conservative views, such as the RAND corporation and the Henry Jackson Society, consistently put forward the view that Islam itself as a culture is a problem. For this reason, Muslims cannot be trusted to make their own minds up about what just governance looks like. We see this in the words of the US diplomat Jeane Kirkpatrick, "The Arab world is the only part of the world where I've been shaken in my conviction that if you let people decide, they will make fundamentally rational choices." Judith Miller's view echoes Kirkpatrick's, "Free elections seem more likely than any other route to produce militant Islamic regimes that are, in fact, inherently antidemocratic."[cl]

Through this epistemological lens, Muslims cannot self-determine – they cannot be left alone to their own devices, for if they do, they will choose incorrectly and so the West must intervene on their behalf. It is instructive to know that in the response to certain types of oppressive conservatism, a form of false paternalism emerges through liberal discourse. In others contexts, such as Apartheid South Africa, Steve Biko was very clear in calling out the lie of liberal concern, one that resonates with my experience as a Muslim:

> *Thus in adopting the line of a nonracial approach, the liberals are playing their old game. They are claiming a "monopoly on intelligence and moral judgement" and setting the pattern and pace for the realisation of the black man's aspirations. They want to remain in good books with both the black and white worlds. They want to shy away from all forms of "extremisms", condemning "white supremacy"*

as being just as bad as "Black Power!". They vacillate between the two worlds, verbalising all the complaints of the blacks beautifully while skilfully extracting what suits them from the exclusive pool of white privileges. But ask them for a moment to give a concrete meaningful programme that they intend adopting, then you will see on whose side they really are. Their protests are directed at and appeal to white conscience, everything they do is directed at finally convincing the white electorate that the black man is also a man and that at some future date he should be given a place at the white man's table.

The myth of integration as propounded under the banner of liberal ideology must be cracked and killed because it makes people believe that something is being done when in actual fact the artificial integrated circles are a soporific on the blacks and provide a vague satisfaction for the guilty-stricken whites. It works on a false premise that because it is difficult to bring people from different races together in this country, therefore achievement of this is in itself a step forward towards the total liberation of the blacks. Nothing could be more irrelevant and therefore misleading. Those who believe in it are living in a fool's paradise.[cli]

When we consider how the alienated and disenfranchised are treated, not just as a minority, but as subjects of epistemologies that seek to determine for us the way that we think, not just what our view of the problem might be. The culturalist or confrontationalist approach is criticised by liberals, who are more accommodationist in their approach. Liberals, seemingly defend Muslims, but from specific readings of Islam. They don't even particularly have a problem with Islam itself, so long as it fits within a specific paradigm of the way western liberal values conceive of religion. As Professor Arun Kundnani points out:

> *Thus, for liberals, Islam is intolerance, racism, and oppression of women. For conservatives, Islam is fanatical, alien, and barbaric. In this mode, Islam is merely the absolute "Other" that enables the construction of a positive image of oneself.[clii]*

Liberals have not set up a clash of civilisations but rather a clash within civilisations – the neo-conservatives promote Judeo-Christian values, and the liberals promote western secular values – but what they both do, is set themselves up in opposition to Islam. Thus the liberals put forth as champions individuals such as Ed Husain and Maajid Nawaz, as enlightened Muslims who will provide Muslims a correctly reformed religion. In that vein, they will even invite Ayaan Hirsi Ali, an ex-Muslim, to participate in debates around Islam's reformation which means that something must be done to help Muslims understand what their place is. This is perhaps best exemplified by the words of the author Martin Amis:

> *The Muslim community will have to suffer until it gets its house in order." What sort of suffering? Not letting them travel. Deportation – further down the road. Curtailing of freedoms. Strip- searching people who look like they're from the Middle East or from Pakistan ... Discriminatory stuff, until it hurts the whole community and they start getting tough with their children.[cliii]*

The liberal defence of Islam, is ultimately constructed as an attack on any aspect of the faith that does not comport to western liberalism. In his introduction to Ahmet Hamdi Tanpinar's excellent science fiction novel 'The Time Regulation Institute', Pankaj Mishra identifies that anxiety that writers such as Tanpinar had with notions of western 'progress' as being a panacea to the problems of the East:

> *The political pursuit of freedom can lead to its eradication on a grand scale. The Time Regulation Institute is to be savored, among other things, for the brilliance of such insights. Tanpinar presciently feared that to embrace the Western conception of progress was to be mentally enslaved by a whole new epistemology, one that compartmentalized knowledge and concealed an instrumental view of human beings as no more than things to be manipulated.*[cliv]

It is through this lens that we can understand Donald J Trump defending Islam from the terrorists in Saudi Arabia, telling his partners in the Muslim world:

> *It is a choice between two futures – and it is a choice America CANNOT make for you. A better future is only possible if your nations drive out the terrorists and extremists. Drive. Them. Out.*
>
> *DRIVE THEM OUT of your places of worship. DRIVE THEM OUT of your communities. DRIVE THEM OUT of your holy land, and DRIVE THEM OUT OF THIS EARTH.*[clv]

Donald J Trump mimics the narrative of almost every leader in the US and UK from Bush and Blair, to Obama and Cameron, to now Trump and May – we will permit Muslims to live with us, providing they accept the terms of reference for what we consider to be acceptable Islam, regardless of what their actual grievances may be. In a 2011 speech given in almost entirely similar language, the former British Prime Minister David Cameron posited the need for a muscular liberalism, one that would be intolerant of intolerance and that would defend Islam. In his critique of the speech, Professor Brian Klug provides an appropriate riposte to the lack of epistemology in Cameron's speech:

> *This brings me to Cameron's first person singular, his "voice": the point from which his words emanate. He says the "young men" in question follow "a completely perverse, warped interpretation of Islam." The question I want to raise is not , "Is he right or is he wrong?" but "Who is he to make this pronouncement?" In what voice does he speak, when he characterises their Islam this way? Taking the podium in Munich, he is speaking as the British prime minister. But is this a ministerial judgement? What kind of judgement is it exactly? Let me suggest a parallel. Consider those religious Jewish settlers in the West Bank who claim the land and attack Palestinian farmers in the name of the Torah and of halachah. Do they follow an interpretation of Judaism that is "completely perverse" and "warped?" If you are asking me, then, speaking as a Jew, my answer is "Yes, they do." But if Cameron gave this answer, my hackles would rise and I would say, "Hang on: who do you think you are that you give an answer to this question? It is not your question." He is, of course, welcome to condemn the settlers in his own name, but not in the name of Judaism. Similarly with Islam and the take on Islam that justifies political violence against civilians: it is not his province. The point is not that what he says is wrong; the*

> *point is that he is the wrong person to be saying it. Yet (and this is crucial) he assumes he can speak with authority for Islam. He takes it for granted, as if it were within his prerogative to distinguish the true Islam from the false, the good from the bad, the goats from the sheep. Is it within his prerogative because he speaks as prime minister? As British? As European? As Christian? As "white?" One thing is certain: he does not speak as a Muslim.[clvi]*

This is what the cultural theorist Gayatri Spivak termed 'epistemic violence'. The violence is carried out against Muslims by both neo-conservatives and neo-liberals is not just physical, through the structural racism of counter-terrorism legislation, policies and wars; it is also the violence that is perpetrated against knowledge itself. So much of this is in translation, it is not just about the translation itself, but who is translating, and what is lost in that process – leading to violence against the original meaning and intention. Lina Mounzer describes this process perfectly:

> *To translate a text is to enter into the most intimate relationship with it possible. It is the translator's body, almost more so than the translator's mind, that is the vessel of transfer. The mind equates words, expressions, deals with techniques and logistics; it is within the body that the real alchemy—mysterious, unnamed and inexplicable—takes place. That alchemy has to do with truth more than signification, that is, the animating force behind signification, which transforms it into meaning, into something that moves. Gayarti Spivak qualifies the act of translation as "erotic," but there is something too gentle about that word to ring true for me. The word*

> *captures the act of surrender, and the*
> *abundantly physical communion with the text,*
> *but there is something messier and bloodier that*
> *is elided. More agonized and agonizing too.*
> *There is a violence in undoing someone's words*
> *and reconstituting them in a vocabulary foreign*
> *to them, a vocabulary of your own choosing.*
> *There is a violence, too, in the way you are—for*
> *long moments—annihilated by the other;*
> *undone in return. Neither the translator nor the*
> *text emerges from the act unscathed.*[clvii]

Knowledge, must be a key site of our resistance, for the terms of reference about the 'Muslim problem' are being set for Muslims outside of Islam. That is not a circumstance that we can afford to continue carrying on, for it leaves faith, people and ideas open to restriction and violence. How can the Muslim know him or herself, when a box is provided within which parameters for thinking are set by external agents? That is not freedom, it is social-engineering.

Laleh Khalili's excellent and detailed assessment of the legacy of western intervention in the world provides us one example of how we can resist faux-epistemologies, by effectively retelling our stories and owning our own narrative. Writing of the impacts of colonialism on the Middle East in 'Time in the Shadows', she explained:

> *Asymmetric warfare was crucial to the conquest*
> *of the Americas, Africa, and Asia. In those*
> *places, asymmetry was not necessarily*
> *engendered by the numeric superiority of the*
> *colonizers, and certainly not in the early years*
> *of the conquest. In fact, in most of the colonized*
> *places, the colonizers were at first numerically*
> *inferior, sometimes dramatically so; what gave*
> *them their military advantage was their access*

> *to superior arms and often savage methods of warfare, their utilization of divide and conquer in aligning with local factions (often via economic incentives), their cunning use of treaties and laws on which they reneged unscrupulously, the immediate establishment of centralized governance regimes and institutions that codified their systems of domination and that in nonsettler colonies were most successful when deployed via local intermediaries or clients, and their capacity for ruthless suppression of any resistance in war or to their new regimes of rule. All that advantage was then veiled in the cloak of "civilization" spun from the weft of law and woof of popular and expert discourse.*[clviii]

You cannot erase the imprints of empire, colonialism, racism and division from our histories, identities and narratives. For us to be true about the world we live in and to understand how it is that we have constructed ourselves as a response, we first need to be honest enough to inject our histories into the present day, as their consequences are real and not imagined. This reminds me of a brilliant sketch by the Muslim Australian comedian Aamer Rahman, where he decimates notions of reverse racism, but also highlights the extent to which structural racism that exists today, is a product of its colonial past:

> *I think there is such a thing asreverse racismand uh... I could be, I could be a reverse racist, if I wanted to, all I would need would be a time machine, right?And what I'd do is I'd get in my time machine, I'd go back in time to before Europe colonized the world, right? And, I'd convince the leaders of Africa, Asia, the Middle East, Central and South America to*

*invade and colonize Europe, right?
Just occupy them, steal their land, resources; set
up some kind of like, I don't know, trans Asian
slave trade where we exported white people to
work on giant rice plantations in China — just
ruin Europe over the course of a couple
centuries so, all their descendants would want
to migrate out and live in places where black
and brown people come from.
But of course, in that time, I'd make sure I set
up systems that privilege black and brown
people at every conceivable social, political and
economic opportunity, and white people would
never have any hope of real self-determination.
Just every couple of decades make up some fake
war as an excuse to go and bomb them back to
the Stone Age and say it's for their own good
because their culture's inferior.
And then just for kicks, subject white people to
colored standards of beauty so they end up
hating the color of their own skin, eyes and
hair.
And if, after hundreds and hundreds and
hundreds of years of that, I got up on stage and
said, "Hey, what's the deal with white people?
Why can't they dance?" That, would bereverse
racism.[clix]*

Rahman is making a serious point in the midst of the
comedy, that you cannot understand a phenomenon
devoid of its complexity. You cannot begin to
understand racism without all of the multi-
generational environmental factors that have led to its
construction, it is about knowledge and narrative. Until
now our narrative has been deprived to us, because the
language by which we can speak is set, and the terms of
reference are established as acts of epistemic violence.

However, I resist this. My second site of resistance will be the knowledge that I own, and the way that I construct that knowledge for the sake of fully understanding the phenomena that impact on my communities. It is a real moment in the autobiography of Frederick Douglass, when he finally understands the value of knowledge and learning, and how it can be emancipatory:

> *"If you give a nigger an inch, he will take an ell. A nigger should know nothing but to obey his master—to do as he is told to do. Learning would spoil the best nigger in the world. Now,"* said he, *"if you teach that nigger (speaking of myself) how to read, there would be no keeping him. It would forever unfit him to be a slave. He would at once become unmanageable, and of no value to his master. As to himself, it could do him no good, but a great deal of harm. It would make him discontented and unhappy."* These words sank deep into my heart, stirred up sentiments within that lay slumbering, and called into existence an entirely new train of thought. It was a new and special revelation, explaining dark and mysterious things, with which my youthful understanding had struggled, but struggled in vain. I now understood what had been to me a most perplexing difficulty—to wit, the white man's power to enslave the black man. It was a grand achievement, and I prized it highly. From that moment, I understood the pathway from slavery to freedom. It was just what I wanted, and I got it at a time when I the least expected it. Whilst I was saddened by the thought of losing the aid of my kind mistress, I was gladdened by the invaluable instruction which, by the merest

accident, I had gained from my master. Though conscious of the difficulty of learning without a teacher, I set out with high hope, and a fixed purpose, at whatever cost of trouble, to learn how to read. The very decided manner with which he spoke, and strove to impress his wife with the evil consequences of giving me instruction, served to convince me that he was deeply sensible of the truths he was uttering. It gave me the best assurance that I might rely with the utmost confidence on the results which, he said, would know from teaching me to read. What he most dreaded, that I most desired. What he most loved, that I most hated. That which to him was a great evil, to be carefully shunned, was to me a great good, to be diligently sought; and the argument which he so warmly urged, against my learning to read, only served to inspire me with a desire and determination to learn. In learning to read, I owe almost as much to the bitter opposition of my master, as to the kindly aid of my mistress. I acknowledge the benefit of both.[clx]

Perhaps the best example I can give of how this has been practised in my life, is through CAGE's fight with the government over the Prevent programme. For years we have been sparring with one another over the impact of the Prevent strategy, the government saying that it helps people from becoming terrorists, CAGE saying that it fuels disenfranchisement through its bad practice and negative consequences on communities.

The reality is, that the odds are stacked against you when dealing with the state. We have no way of truly breaking through their walls of national security secrecy in order to gain any real data or statistics (except through leaks), and we are always reliant on the brave survivor families (who are in the minority) who actually feel strong enough to come forward to talk publically about the way the state has treated them through Prevent.

About 2 years ago, we decided to change direction. I asked one simple question to the team: how does the government know how 'radicalisation' works? In so many ways, this seemed like a stupid question. After all, for 15 years the government had been talking about fighting terrorism and combatting extremism, but how did they really know? Yes, we know that they rely on 'experts' to help make their case, but still, they have to base their policy on some form of formal process? In other words, there was a knowledge base somewhere in existence that provided information about how the government came to its conclusions about whether an individual was "prone to commit an act of terrorism", and so instead of looking at impacts, we decided we would resist at the site of knowledge.

In pursuit of the how, we had to draw a line back from their conclusions. As I mentioned in the chapter on the System and Collaborators, the government produced a list of 22 factors that they felt indicated that someone was at risk of radicalisation and on the pathways towards terrorism. These factors were being used in training around the country in the government's e-learning programme, with Prevent police officers and vetted individuals involved in delivering the training. These factors were sold to the public as scientific produced through the government's policy document the 'Channel Vulnerability Assessment (CVA) Framework'. Still, this document did not give us any further information, that was until we found another version of the document online that stated that the CVA was based on the Extremism Risk Guidance 22+ study.

Twenty-two factors are presented, and when we

found a reference to a study that is talking about guidance 22+, we realised we had finally found the science. Or at least we thought that was the case, until we began our search for it. We looked everywhere online, in libraries and finally resorted to calling the National Offenders Management Service who were responsible for the production of the report – they explained that they could not share this study as it was a matter of national security.

Until this day we still have not seen the study, but what we did find, was a journal article describing the study. This journal, was so conceptually and methodologically flawed, that it resulted in CAGE producing a detailed response with the assistance of 19 senior psychologists, academics and experts around terrorism and political violence.

The report itself caused so much concern in the academic community that it resulted in 160 academics signing a joint letter in the Guardian with the Royal College of Psychiatry making their own intervention to ask questions around the lack of transparency and pseudo-science in the process.

What CAGE successfully managed to do, was to take on the government's epistemological basis for the claim that there is something called a 'pre-crime' space, by effectively showing that such terms should be relegated only to the imagination of Philip K Dick in his 'Minority Report'.

This incident highlights how important knowledge is. We should not simply accept generalised assumptions that are made within the security context, especially, without a thorough investigation of what the terms being used are, and what science or knowledge base underpins those assumptions. By only ever dealing with the consequences of policy, we fail to realise the true problem that we face: that although we are able to highlight wrong doing, we cannot make the case that it is structurally wrong unless we question the 'how' of the policy to begin with.

Knowledge, as a site of resistance, permits us to re-own our identity, as well through language and our narrative. Faux-knowledge, when applied to communities, serves only as a weapon to harm them, and as Ta-Nehisi Coates writes to his son:

> *"It is hard to face this. But all our phrasing—race relations, racial chasm, racial justice, racial profiling, white privilege, even white supremacy—serves to obscure that racism is a visceral experience, that it dislodges brains, blocks airways, rips muscle, extracts organs, cracks bones, breaks teeth. You must never look away from this. You must always remember that the sociology, the history, the economics, the graphs, the charts, the regressions all land, with great violence, upon the body."[clxi]*

Community

I have been very fortunate in my work to have alongside me colleagues and comrades from whom I learn so much. Perhaps the single most important gift that I was given was in the form of tutelage under Dr Scharlette Holdman, the person who helped to discover the concept of mitigation against the death penalty in the US.[clxii] Scharlette taught me about how to interview witnesses without interviewing them, about how to resist the temptation to be expedient with investigations, but most of all, she taught me how to recognise and work with survivors of trauma.

Trauma has layers that are sometimes difficult to unpick – it exists in the mind as well as in the body. Often, when I am describing how trauma affects the body, I use the example of men. When we, as men, watch someone hit in the private parts, perhaps on TV, our instinct is to lurch forward and to press down near our groin area, as if we had exactly the same feeling as the person we were watching. This is not purely out of sympathy or empathy, this is the body's physiological response to a previous trauma that was inflicted on it. Imagine then what it is like for a survivor of torture to speak about their experience, as the person conducting the interview, you are effectively asking them to bring back painful memories, but you are effectively asking them to harm themselves again as the body responds in synchrony to protecting itself from the descriptions the survivor is giving.

One of the books I most value on trauma is 'Trauma and Recovery: The aftermath of violence – from domestic abuse to political terror' by Judith Herman. The book charts the history of science on trauma, but also brings it into the contemporary world. We learn about coercive control and the way in which the logics between sexual violence are often similar to that of political violence, particularly when carried out by the state.

The key to the book for me is the second half of the title, the aspect of recovery. For Herman there are three stages: safety, narrative and community – needing to work sequentially in that order. You cannot expect for trauma to end until safety has been reached. Once the person is at safety, you cannot expect them to reclaim their identity until they have come to terms with their narrative. Finally, you cannot expect them to find normality in life, until they find meaning in the communities around them. Much of what Herman writes is about the individual, and how individual trauma is treated, and in that sense, I am interested in the community, the suspect community, and how it develops layers of trauma as stories of abuse travel between them.

The above two sections on language and knowledge provide some insights into the second stage, about narrative and how to recapture narrative from those who have denied it to you. What does safety look like in the UK and US, and I don't just mean safety here from police brutality or hate crimes, I mean also from the excesses of the state? How can suspect communities, such as African-Americans overcome their trauma of Michael Brown, Trayvon Martin, Tamir Rice, Sandra Bland, Philando Castle and the names go on? How can Muslim communities overcome the spate of killings (and in one potential case a lynching) in the US, and in the UK how can they end the structural violence of the entire apparatus of the state from engaging in systemic discrimination?

Perhaps one of the most famous responses to such forms of violence came from Malcolm X:

> *There is nothing in our book, the Qur'ān, that teaches us to suffer peacefully. Our religion teaches us to be intelligent. Be peaceful, be courteous, obey the law, respect everyone; but if someone lays a hand on you, send him to the cemetery. That's a good religion.*[clxiii]

I have to admit here that like Malcolm, I am not a pacifist. I do believe that every single human being has the right to resist in order to feel safe from the threats they face. I also do not think he was promoting violence for the sake of violence – which is where justice lies. Human beings have an inherent right to protect themselves to feel safe, but not to engage in violence when there is no threat. What is the threat though? What are the boundaries of the threats we face? James Baldwin, chose to critique his friend Malcolm X, but in doing so actually went further in his assessment of the problem:

> *Whether in private debate or in public, any*

attempt I made to explain how the Black Muslim movement came about, and how it achieved such force, was met with a blankness that revealed the little connexion that the liberals' attitudes have with their perceptions of their lives, or even their knowledge - revealed, in fact, that they could deal with the Negro as a symbol or a victim but had no sense of him as a man. When Malcolm X, who is considered the movement's second-in-command, and heir apparent, points out that the cry of 'violence' was not raised, for example, when the Israelis fought to regain Israel, and, indeed, is raised only when black men indicate that they will fight for their rights, he is speaking the truth. The conquests of England, every single one of them bloody, are part of what Americans have in mind when they speak of England's glory. In the United States, violence and heroism have been made synonymous except when it comes to blacks, and the only way to defeat Malcolm's point is to concede it and then ask oneself why this is so. Malcolm's statement is not answered by references to the triumphs of the N.A.A.C.P, the more particularly since very few liberals have any notion of how long, how costly, and how heartbreaking a task it is to gather the evidence that one can carry into court, or how long such court battles take. Neither is it answered by references to the student sit-in movement, if only because not all Negroes are students and not all of them live in the South. I, in any case, certainly refuse to be put in the position of denying the truth of Malcolm's statements simply because I disagree with his conclusions, or in order to pacify the liberal conscience. Things are as bad as the Muslims

> *say they are - in fact, they are worse, and the*
> *Muslims do not help matters - but there is no*
> *reason that black men should be expected to be*
> *more patient, more forebearing, more far-seeing*
> *than whites; indeed, quite the contrary.*[clxiv]

Baldwin is as incisive as he is scathing in his critique. He makes clear that the problem with the concept of violence is undermined by liberal attitudes. Those who exceptionalise certain types of violence and normalise others. He goes further: he identifies the problem with non-violence too – making the claim that more is expected of black lives in terms of forbearance than expected of any other community. James Baldwin takes issue with the approach that Malcolm X takes, but goes further in identifying the structural problems in relation to the way that resistance is formulated. What then of the lives of others? As I discussed in the chapter on witnessing and community, I have obligations to those around me and even those further afield.

When the Prophet Muḥammad established the city of Madinah, there were some Muslims who remained in Makkah[clxv]; they were not able or permitted to migrate, such as Ibn 'Abbas and his father, who specifically prayed to Allāh, "O, our Lord, bring us forth from this town, Mecca, whose people are evildoers, through unbelief, and appoint for us a protector from You, to take charge of our affair, and appoint for us from You a helper."[clxvi] This supplication was heard by Allāh, and referenced within the revealed verse:

> *Why should you not fight in God's cause and for*
> *those oppressed men, women and children who*
> *cry out, 'Lord, rescue us from this town whose*
> *people are oppressors! By your grace, give us a*
> *protector and give us a helper!'?*[clxvii]

What are the obligations when such a call is made? I

look at Syria – I have seen videos of children literally begging the international community to come to rescue them from the incessant shelling of Bashar al-Assad, and yet I do not move to action. I am trained in Law. Would bringing legal challenges be my contribution to fulfilling the cry of the oppressed? James Baldwin is right, the challenges take too long – by the time you go through the system so many lives are lost. What of sit-ins? He's right again, sit-ins only work for some, otherwise we would be conducting sit-ins all of the time.

When I think about safety, it is difficult to imagine what that might look like, because there doesn't seem to be a solution that can bring a resolution to the multitude of problems that we see.

What I do know, is that I am a Muslim, and with that comes expectations. I have expectations of myself, for my community, and ultimately everything comes back to expectations that I must fulfil before Allāh. Thinking about my resistance and safety in that regard, my resistance must be conditional to my situation. Safety is needed for people in Syria, and the Syrian people are fighting for that, they are literally putting their lives on the line there, as they are in Palestine, Kashmir and Burma, and so many other countries and contexts around the world. I am based in the UK. I have a law degree, a masters in law, can read and write and have networks that are able to assist me – so perhaps that is the starting point of my situating myself in relation to the injustices that I see.

In other words, I am someone who has been given specific privileges by Allāh, and I owe it to the privileges I have been given to use them to maximum effect. Surely that is the point? If it is understood for the Muslim, that your rizq (provision) on this Earth is a determined thing, and so that all that you learnt, all the privileges in life you received were divinely given, then the only conclusion one can draw, is about pushing those privileges to their maximum point of altruism and ultimately sincerity back to Allāh.

It is the only way that I can conceive of managing these multiple obligations.

I can see the draw of violence, of fighting for the sake of a cause for young people. There is a sense of justice and actual physical help, but perhaps that is not what Allāh wants from us all specifically? Surely the most grateful act to Allāh, is to recognise what He has brought into my life, and then to turn that into something that will honour Him and those who are without.

Terrorism or political violence, as a methodology, has never come into my frame of thinking. It is nihilistic and achieves nothing other than to divide, and to allow others to increase authoritarianism – this is not a solution. I find myself agreeing with Ernesto Che Guevara regarding terrorism as a tool:

> *...terrorism, a measure that is generally ineffective and indiscriminate in its results, since it often makes victims of innocent people and destroys a large number of lives that would be valuable to the revolution.*[clxviii]

Safety is achieved through resistance, and resistance is contextual. For black lives, safety may be achieved through moving in larger groups, wearing body cameras (although that isn't working), doing anything that will turn the system's gaze on the police, rather than them. For those in Palestine and Syria, their response will also vary according to the immediate predicament and circumstance, and they will find righteousness in what they do. For me, I remain hopeful in my fellow countrymen. Yes, the system is stacked against you, but I meet too many good people to give up on the notion that change is a dream that we will always wake up from. I find that even as far back as 1553, Etienne de la Boetie understood this perfectly well:

> *By this time it should be evident that liberty once lost, valor also perishes. A subject people shows neither gladness nor eagerness in combat: its men march sullenly to danger almost as if in bonds, and stultified; they do not feel throbbing within them that eagerness for liberty which engenders scorn of peril and imparts readiness to acquire honor and glory by a brave death amidst one's comrades. Among free men there is competition as to who will do most, each for the common good, each by himself, all expecting to share in the misfortunes of defeat, or in the benefits of victory; but an enslaved people loses in addition to this warlike courage, all signs of enthusiasm, for their hearts are degraded, submissive, and incapable of any great deed. Tyrants are well aware of this, and, in order to degrade their subjects further, encourage them to assume this attitude and make it instinctive.[clxix]*

Finding safety means resisting. Safety can never truly take place in an environment where authoritarianism is present, as the relationship is tenuous. Even if you act as a modern day Korah, you are always subject to the whims of the government or regime, and so these fraudulent alliances built off the backs of the oppressed, can never be seen as being what Judith Herman considered to be safety. Rather, it is in fact, part of the trauma of the community. However, even in the most difficult of circumstances, human beings have the ability to reconstruct themselves, to change their own status as they seek to overcome their oppression. Herman provides the example of political prisoners conducting hunger strikes as one example:

> *Political prisoners who are aware of the methods of coercive control devote particular attention to maintaining their sense of autonomy. One form of resistance is refusing to comply with petty demands or to accept rewards. The hunger strike is the ultimate expression of this resistance. Because the prisoner voluntarily subjects himself to greater deprivation than that willed by his captor, he affirms his sense of integrity and self-control. The psychologist Joel Dimsdale describes a woman prisoner in the Nazi concentration camps who fasted on Yom Kippur in order to prove that her captors had not defeated her.[clxx]*

So far, this discussion has largely been restricted to the individual attempting to find safety, or attempting others to find safety. My thesis though, is that the last site of resistance is community, or to be more accurate networks of communities. It is the coming together of people in whatever circumstances they are in, in order to unite beyond their difficulties. I am reminded of the actions taken by Ahmed Errachidi while he was detained at Guantanamo Bay, Cuba. Having been in a process of resisting against the prison authorities and coming unstuck each time, he developed a strategy of resistance that required those around him to rally behind an idea communally:

> *Shouting through the walls, each sharing his opinion, we debated the best way of staging our protest. I'd already been working on an idea for a few weeks - pacing my cell, three steps one way, three steps the other, figuring out my reasoning - so I was prepared. I proposed that we rip up our orange shirts.*

Since the main thrust of our protest was to put an end to the punishment of having our clothes forcibly removed, this must have sounded like a peculiar idea. But I laid out my arguments in a methodical manner, I told my fellows that one of the reasons we were prohibited from removing our clothes was because they were visible and helped the soldiers to identify us. If, I argued, we managed to get the bulk of the prison population to join in the removal and destruction of up to five hundred shirts this would not only confuse them but also send a strong signal about our refusal to put up with punishments, and it would undermine the camp authorities who'd given us the orange kit. Since, I continued, it was compulsory for them to clothe us (I told my fellow prisoners that this was written into the Geneva Convention - I didn't know if it was but thought it might be), a prisoner being escorted to interrogation or clinic without a shirt would be an embarrassment to the army. Although we never met them we knew journalists and their like paid frequent visits to the prison and if they were to see us dressed only in our trousers this would make a huge impression. The orange clothes were also a visible sign that we were their prisoners: by removing our shirts we would be sending the administration a message that we were no longer prepared to be their captives. And finally, I argued that if every one of us tore up our shirts at the same time, and if we then tore up any new shirts issued to us, they'd have a serious problem, not least because the Pentagon would start asking why they were spending so much money on shirts.[clxxi]

Necessity is the mother of all inventions, and Errachidi's strategy drove home the protest for the men, yes, bringing them into conflict with the prison administration, but at the same time nullifying the administration's power – particularly as it was an action that was taken collectively. By working together, they forced a change in their conditions of confinement, where they were afforded some semblance of the respect they were due.

We can take hope from this example. Going back to the chapter on the modalities of oppression –by coming together, we reverse that power that authority has. As Angela Davis informs us:

> *But there's a message there for everyone and it is that people can unite, that democracy from below can challenge oligarchy, that imprisoned migrants can be freed, that fascism can be overcome, and that equality is emancipatory.*[clxxii]

Who should come together, and under what basis? Within Islam there are both theological and political differences with other religions and sects – is this what stands as a barrier to collective action against oppression and tyranny? But if your house is on fire, it is literally burning to the ground, then stopping to fix a misplaced picture frame is the equivalent of refusing to cooperate on issues of justice when there is a theological difference. This cooperation becomes tricky though when a particular group or sect chooses to collaborate with the state's immoral policies, and undermine the rights of the communities, but that does not mean that their rights should not be defended.

Islamophobia is structural racism, and so it makes no difference to the immigration officer, or the police officer which religious tradition you come from, you are still treated as a potential threat. I want us to acknowledge, that when an Ahmadi place of worship is burnt down, or a Sikh is beaten or killed in the street for being perceived to be Muslim, or an innocent non-Muslim man like Jean Charles de Menezes is shot twelve times in the back of the head, these are all manifestations of Islamophobia. We should not judge the act by the person harmed, but by the intent of the one who carried out the abuse. We must always remember, that when British police officers killed de Menezes, their honest belief was that they were killing a Muslim.

Recognising our points of intersection. We are all subject to mass surveillance, we are all subject to strict controls when we fly in and out of our countries, and we are in danger of having our digital life intruded on by the state. In that regard, Angela Davis has been at the forefront of establishing connections that others are unwilling to do. She tells us that there is no fighting against racism, unless we are willing to stand up for the plight of the Palestinian people. This passage from her 'Freedom is a Constant Struggle' anthology presents these ideas perfectly, as she highlights the way in which just as there is a best practice of abuse, we need to develop a best practice of resistance:

> *The militarization of the police leads us to think about Israel and the militarization of the police there—if only the images of the police and not of the demonstrators had been shown, one might have assumed that Ferguson [Missouri] was Gaza. I think that it is important to recognize the extent to which, in the aftermath of the advent of the war on terror, police departments all over the US have been equipped with the means to allegedly "fight terror."*[clxxiii]

The consistent theme throughout my reflections in

this book, circle back to the centrality of community in resistance. It is ultimately the place from which we can locate the fulcrum of our virtuous disobedience. Without it, we cannot ever hope to move forward. Each of us has a personal relationship with our own ethics, dictating how we behave, but it is when we act in community, to subvert the accepted notions of behaviour, that we will be able to translate the change that occurs personally, to one that can occur societally.

Patience on Truth

A Virtue Of Disobedience

"We are not content with negative obedience, nor even with the most abject submission. When finally you surrender to us, it must be of your own free will. We do not destroy the heretic because he resists us; so long as he resists us we never destroy him. We convert him, we capture his inner mind, we reshape him. We burn all evil and all illusion out of him; we bring him over to our side, not in appearance, but genuinely, heart and soul."
[George Orwell – 1984]

"He shook his head. "These things frighten people. It's best not to talk about them."
"But, Dad, that's like . . . like ignoring a fire in the living room because we're all in the kitchen, and, besides, house fires are too scary to talk about."
"Don't warn Joanne or any of your other friends," he said. "Not now. I know you think you're right, but you're not doing anyone any good. You're just panicking people.""
[Octavia Butler – Parable of the Sower]

"'We know all the damn silly things we've done for a thousand years, and as long as we know that and always have it around where we can see it, some day we'll stop making the goddam funeral pyres and jumping into the middle of them. We pick up a few more people that remember, every generation,'...
...'Come on now, we're going to build a mirror-factory first and put out nothing but mirrors for the next year and take a long look into them.'"
[Ray Bradbury – Fahrenheit 451]

The Prophet Muḥammad, may peace and blessings be upon him, stood with his army with his arms extended before him, stretching to the skies. He understood one truth that Islam itself was facing an existential crisis, one that it had not faced until that moment. With him, stood 312 soldiers, against them over a thousand of the enemy. They were less well equipped than their opponents, but had belief in their hearts. The invocation that the Prophet made, was to ask for Allāh's help for if they lost that day, there would be none left on the Earth who would worship Him alone.

When we speak of a national emergency situation, I cannot think of a single moment in Islam that might warrant such a claim to the extent that this battle, the Battle of Badr was. Had the Muslims lost on that day, there would be no Islam for us to speak of, let alone believe in.

The Prophet was concerned about the movements of his enemy, so he had sent forward scouts to find a caravan they were looking for, and to conduct reconnaissance on their enemy's location. 'Urwah bin al-Zubayr narrates a situation that takes place during this time:

> "Upon approaching Badr, the Messenger of Allāh sent `Ali bin Abi Talib, Sa`d bin Abi Waqqas, Az-Zubayr bin Al-`Awwam and several other Companions to spy on the pagans. They captured two boys, a servant of Bani Sa`id bin Al-`As and a servant of Bani Al-Hajjaj, while they were bringing water for Quraysh. So they brought them to the Messenger of Allāh, but found him praying. The Companions started interrogating the boys, asking them to whom they belonged. Both of them said that they were employees bringing water for

Quraysh (army). The Companions were upset with that answer, since they thought that the boys belonged to Abu Sufyan (who was commanding the caravan). So they beat the two boys vehemently, who said finally that they belonged to Abu Sufyan. Thereupon Companions left them alone. When the Prophet ended the prayer, he said,

"When they tell you the truth you beat them, but when they lie you let them go. They have said the truth, by Allāh! They belong to the Quraysh."[clxxiv]

This narration is very important from a number of perspectives. It shows the significance of this encounter to the Muslims, as all the leaders of the Quraysh attended to take part in the fighting. However, I am left wondering about what seems to be the Prophet's criticism of the efficacy of torture. In my mind, the information the men received on beating the two young men from Quraysh, was false because they had said whatever they could to make the beating stop.

The majority of my adult life has been lived in a state of exception, where we are consistently told that we need emergency legislation and policy in order to avert an existential crisis. We need temporary exceptions to the Rule of Law, in order to protect freedoms and our way of life. If ever, there was a moment in the history of Islam, where the Prophet might make an exception to the Rule of Law for the sake of expediency, it was this one. This moment, was an actual existential crisis, and instead of resorting to torturing these boys, the Prophet spoke against it. In my own reflections on this incident, that regardless of the circumstance, regardless of what threat you might fear – torture cannot be used as a weapon of interrogation.

In the light of models of resistance for the sake of a

virtue of disobedience, initially I was going to include truth-speaking as a separate site of resistance, but I changed my mind. Truth and truth-speaking are not just sites of resistance; the truth represents our constant. It is the constant in our equation of resistance. Without the truth, we cannot seek to undermine authority and displace tyranny, for it is despots who deal mostly in the currency of lies.

I recall sitting with a trauma survivor in the Middle East. He told me his story of how he had been abused for thirteen years in a solitary confinement cell by the Americans. This man's spirit and courage to survive was beyond all comprehension, and I could not understand how he managed to keep his sanity in that time. That was, until I realised this man's commitment to the truth. He described to me a situation where his lawyers required him to play up his ill-treatment for the sake of helping them to make their case:

> *I don't know how to describe the choking. It was like I was dying. I could not breathe. I could not even cough as my mouth was closed from the socks and the tapes. During the choking I felt like I was going to die, not that I felt I was near death, but I was panicked into thinking it. If they continued, I would have stopped breathing. It was so intense. I accepted it. This was a test from Allāh and I do not have any psychological problems. I will say this, I will not exaggerate, or say things for the sake of making my case more strong. One of my lawyers was asking me questions about my psychological problems, and after my reply, he said that this isn't really the right answer. I said no, truth is always right. I believe the benefit of telling the truth is much more benefit to me than any obvious advantage of lying. Lying is short lived.*

That does not excuse them of their responsibility of what they have done. Choking is no fun.[clxxv]

I think a lot about his phrase, 'lying is short lived', and indeed it is, which is why more than anything else, the truth has to be the mast to which we staple all of our other forms of resistance – otherwise we not only undermine ourselves in the short term, but undermine our movement in the long-term.

I really have no desire to throw a friend under the bus for the sake of making a point, but I am sure that Phil Shiner will agree that we can take some lessons from his case. Shiner was an excellent lawyer who worked furiously for the sake of those who had been wronged by the state, particularly in Iraq where he was suing the UK armed forces for abuses they carried out against the Iraqi population. Unfortunately Shiner cut corners, leading to false claims being made due to the information he was receiving and passing on. Of course, it is hard enough to see a lawyer who was known for his human rights record be struck off from his profession, but the damage went much deeper, as the tabloid press picked up on the line of litigation against the armed services and called them all into question, bringing an end to all the accountability processes. For the disenfranchised, being beyond reproach, is our only option. Maya Angelou understood this even as a child – that she had to be more certain of her facts than anyone else – when she reflects on her childhood in 'I Know Why the Caged Bird Sings':

In the school itself I was disappointed to find that I was not the most brilliant or even nearly the most brilliant student. The white kids had better vocabularies than I and, what was more appalling, less fear in the classrooms. They never hesitated to hold up their hands in response to a teacher's question; even when they

> *were wrong they were wrong aggressively,*
> *while I had to be certain about all my facts*
> *before I dared to call attention to myself.*[clxxvi]

People of colour, and those resisting the state do not have the luxury of cutting corners or uttering lies in the course of our defence. We cannot afford to make mistakes as we know what mistakes cost us. The South African comedian Trevor Noah brings this point home well in his segment on the Philando Castile case:

> *People said there is a simple solution to police*
> *shootings just give the police body cameras...film*
> *everything...then there'll be no question about*
> *what happened. And black people have already*
> *taken that initiative, thanks to cell phones every*
> *black person has a bodycam.*

> *Black people have been saying for years, give us*
> *an indictment, just give us an indictment. You*
> *know, just get us in front of a jury...just in front*
> *of a jury of our peers, of our fellow citizens.*
> *We'll show them the video, the evidence, and*
> *then they will see it and justice will be served.*
> *And finally black people get there and it's like*
> *wait what? Nothing?*

> *You hear the stories and you like watch that.*
> *Forget race, are we watching the same video?*
> *The video where a law abiding young man*
> *follows the officer's instruction to the letter of*
> *the law and was killed regardless. People*
> *watched that video and then voted to acquit.*
> *And the saddest thing is that wasn't the only*
> *video that they watched.*[clxxvii]

He first sets out the way in which structural discrimination takes place against Castile, so that we understand the environment in which we are operating. However, it is his next point that drives the truth home when he speaks of Castile's girlfriend and her reaction:

> *'You shot four bullets into him...sir' It's f***ing mind blowing that Diamond Reynolds has just seen her boyfriend shot in front of her. She still have the presence of mind to be deferential to the policeman. In that moment the cop has panicked, but clearly black people never forget their training. Still in that moment a black person is saying sir, I respect you...sir...I understand what I need to do...sir.*[clxxviii]

People of colour know that they cannot make mistakes, for they are punished in a way that others are not. Those in the resistance are punished in a way that others are not. So we have to be serious about what it means to make mistakes in our movements, because the consequences can be far reaching and extremely damaging. I am a witness to this, having made my own share of errors which have come back to bite not only me, but the organisation I represent. Focusing too much on holding the state to account, I didn't take into account the feelings of the victims of Jihadi John, the man who executed dozens of ISIS victims, when I described the man I once knew, as a 'beautiful man'. Regardless of the difficulties he had been put through, it was important to take into account the suffering of others, and on this occasion I failed to do so, as I recognised in an article I wrote for Middle East Eye.[clxxix]

My colleagues at CAGE and I felt the issue so important, that we commissioned an external review of how we handled the press conference, leading to many lessons learned that we would implement in the future.[clxxx] Although demonised, fortunately we still have relevance with our own communities, but not without great effort by the state to drive a wedge between us and our support base. The pressure to condemn on the terms of those who fear Muslims is great, and it is difficult to understand why we must resist that urge. I carried the weight of my refusal to condemn, and it was on reading Yassir Morsi's 'Radical Skin, Moderate Masks', that I felt someone finally understand where we were coming from. On being invited to a TV show to discuss ISIS, on the taxi ride to the studio, Morsi considered what he would do if he was asked to condemn, a process that I have through almost verbatim:

> *While passing through the leafy and affluent area of Melbourne's South Yarra, around the bends of the river, I began to rehearse my responses to potential questions. I could easily guess what they would ask of me. I could easily guess what my responsibility as a Muslim, academic and community activist would be. While rehearsing, I found I was overfocused on negating the jihadist. I had committed myself to avoiding this trap and made a person pledge to not denounce ISIS. I came to this conclusion not because I support or have sympathies for their cause. My politics and their have nothing in common. I wanted to sabotage what I saw as a liberal society's and media's insistent call for a collective Muslim responsibility to condemn, to distance and explain ourselves.[clxxxi]*

The detentions of leading figures is a tactic of repression that has often been used in the past in order to undermine the truth-speakers. Angela Davis, in many ways the conscience of the civil rights movement in America, was arrested and detained for her activism, with lies being spread against her in order to undermine her ability to lead her communities:

> *And I should say parenthetically, when I learned about this in May, I remembered when*

> *I was placed on the Ten Most Wanted. I didn't make the Ten Most Wanted terrorist list, I think they didn't have one at that time, but I made the Ten Most Wanted criminal list. And I was represented as armed and dangerous. And you know one of the things I remember thinking to myself was, what is this all about? What could I possibly do? And then I realized it wasn't about me at all; it wasn't about the individual at all. It was about sending a message to large numbers of people whom they thought they could discourage from involvement in the freedom struggles at that time.*[clxxxii]

Angela Davis speaks often about Assata Shakur, the Black Panther activist also being put on the FBI most wanted list, but in Shakur's case, the most wanted terrorist list. It is these actions that result in the state's hand of repression becoming apparent. Rather than allow for the process of democratic accountability to take place, they undermine their opponents by putting them through a process of maligning them and undermining their ability to function. With the advent of even more modern technology than we have ever had, we live in a time when even the concept of imprisonment has taken on wider and more significant meanings, in many ways the surveillance society has established an open air Benthamite panopticon.[clxxxiii] Within the context of warfare Grégoire Chamayou summarises this point well in his book 'Drone Theory':

> *Drones are indeed petrifying. They inflict mass terror upon entire populations. It is this—over and above the deaths, the injuries, the destruction, the anger, and the grieving—that is the effect of permanent lethal surveillance: it amounts to a psychic imprisonment within a perimeter no longer defined by bars, barriers,*

> *and walls, but by the endless circling of flying*
> *watchtowers up above.*[clxxxiv]

Drones terrify. It is part of the function that they serve, but as aptly described by Chamayou, they have a much deeper significance in that they create an environment of fear. Those on the ground do not only live with one eye on the sky, but also with a suspicious eye on those around them, knowing that collaborators work in tandem with operators to identify targets – more often than not incorrectly. The surveillance state presents a similar function now through its ability to gather large amounts of data and extract information through the exceptional powers that have been permitted in the West since 11 September 2001.

In the UK, for example, if you travel through any port either by plane, train or ferry, you can be stopped under schedule 7 of the Terrorism Act 2000 and questioned. Answering questions is not just mandatory; by refusing to answer you have committed a terrorism offence and can be prosecuted and sentenced for up to three months in prison for non-compliance. The statistics that we know of these stops, is that almost 50,000 individuals are stopped under the powers each year, with often people of colour being specifically targeted by the powers.[clxxxv] Although they do not collect data about Muslims, we know anecdotally from the road shows we carry out around the UK, that this is a common experience for most Muslims.[clxxxvi]

What of the 'made it' Muslims? We do, after all, have celebrities among our midst who in many ways are considered to have a shroud of acceptability and respectability that makes them immune to this type of profiling treatment. The Muslim British-Pakistani actor and musician, Riz Ahmed, writes about his experience at the schedule 7 stop. Admittedly, initially he did not have the fame of starring roles in 'The Reluctant

Fundamentalist', 'Four Lions', 'The Night Of' and most prominently 'Star Wars: Rogue One', but still, his main experience occurred after having picked up a Silver Bear and the Berlin Film Festival for his role in 'The Road to Guantanamo':

> *My first film was in this mode, Michael Winterbottom's The Road to Guantanamo. It told the story of a group of friends from Birmingham who were illegally detained and tortured there. When it won a prestigious award at the Berlin Film Festival, we were euphoric. For those who saw it, the inmates went from orange jumpsuits to human beings.*

> *But airport security hadn't got the memo. Returning to the glamour of Luton Airport after our festival win, ironically-named 'British intelligence officers' frog-marched me to an unmarked room where they insulted, threatened, then attacked me.*

> *'What kinda film you making? Did you become an actor to further the Muslim struggle?' an officer screamed, twisting my arm to the point of snapping.*

> *The question is disturbing not only because it endangers artistic expression, but because it suggests our security services don't quite grasp the nature of the terror threat we all face. A presentation outlining Al-Qaeda's penchant for 'theatrical' attacks may have been taken a little literally. Their suspicion of thespians may also explain why those Guantanamo Bay prisoners are so goddamn photogenic.* [clxxxvii]

Ahmed writes about the necklaces of identity that are forced on us, that we wear them around our necks like badges, ones that constrict on the neck as they apply the layers that profile us. I prefer to think of this necklace as a noose, a symbol that takes on new meaning when I think of Ben Keita, the young Muslim boy in the US found hanging from a tree that was suspiciously too high for him to access on his own – the FBI are still investigating the circumstances of his death.[clxxxviii] Whether the lynching is physical or metaphorical, there are nooses that exist that we must encounter, some of which are tied around us at ports.

In 2016 I was travelling with my colleague at CAGE, Muhammad Rabbani while we were working on the case of a torture survivor who requested our assistance to hold his torturers to account. I had other business to attend to and so Rabbani returned home to London before me. The next thing I knew, a colleague from the CAGE office was calling me to inform me that Rabbani had been arrested under schedule 7 for failure to disclose his passwords when demanded by the police. Rabbani explained to them that as he had client confidential information, he would not be able release the passwords and so accepted that he would be arrested and later charged for not complying.

For years we have been speaking of challenging the extreme intrusiveness of Schedule 7[clxxxix] - it is beyond unconscionable - and Rabbani has shown us all the way by refusing to comply with unreasonable demands, especially as he was under no suspicion. Writing of his experience before his charge, Muhammad Rabbani wrote in an opinion piece for Al Jazeera:

> *During a Schedule 7 detainment a person may be shown photographs of other individuals and asked to give information about them. They often have to face unfounded, fearful allegations of being linked to "terrorism". It is nothing short of injustice and intimidation. This has broad implications for people who need to protect their*

data.

> *This case is not only about me or CAGE. If I give in, this has broad implications for others who want to protect similar relationships and ethics in the face of an encroaching security state. For this reason, my case will set a crucial precedent not just for Muslims, but for all society.*[cxc]

This laudatory stance taken by my colleague is not new. In fact it very much echoes the stances that have been taken by many of our heroes throughout history. This is the path of those who desire peace and justice, and so are willing to put themselves on the line for the sake of achieving those goals:

> *I submit that an individual who breaks a law that conscience tells him is unjust, and who willingly accepts the penalty of imprisonment in order to arouse the conscience of the community over its injustice, is in reality expressing the highest respect for law.*[cxci]

[Martin Luther King Jr]

> *If the machine of government is of such a nature that it requires you to be the agent of injustice to another, then, I say, break the law.*[cxcii]

[Henry David Thoreau]

Imprisonment is preferable to allowing for injustices to take place. This is the ultimate reality for those who choose to resist tyranny. This does not mean that one disobeys every law; the purpose of disrupting laws that are unconscionable, is to raise the spectre of their immorality. Stealing from a shop because counter-terrorism legislation is repressive, does not make any sense, the law that is out of synchrony with moral life should be the target of any resistance.

The story of the Prophet Joseph perhaps provides the clearest indication of this notion of imprisonment for the sake of principle. Joseph, who was described as being incredibly handsome, was placed in a predicament of accepting the advances of the most powerful women in Egypt or face imprisonment over false charges. The prayer that the Prophet Joseph invokes, has been one that is recited by thousands of prisoners who have been detained on false grounds for centuries. It is one I recited myself while imprisoned in an Israeli cell in 2005:

> *He said, "My Lord, prison is more to my liking than that to which they invite me. And if You do not avert from me their plan, I might incline toward them and [thus] be of the ignorant."*[cxciii]

The Prophet Joseph spent years in prison, and despite his assistance to fellow prisoners, he is largely forgotten about. That is, until the Minister of Egypt is in need of his ability to interpret dreams. Joseph's response is really quite exceptional:

> *And the king said, "Bring him to me." But when the messenger came to him, [Joseph] said, "Return to your master and ask him what is the case of the women who cut their hands. Indeed, my Lord is Knowing of their plan."*[cxciv]

Joseph is given the perfect opportunity to leave prison. Imagine after years of unlawful detention, someone comes and says that yes you can leave, you are being called by the head of the state, and he needs your help. I think many of us would probably leave. Joseph isn't just anyone though, he refuses the order for him to leave and tells the messenger to ask the minister to first resolve the false allegations that were levelled against him.

When I think of this story, and the degree of principle that was exercised, I do think of Rabbani, but

I also think of all those Guantanamo Bay detainees who were told they could leave the prison if they signed a form that said they were al-Qaeda – these men refused, saying that they would rather stay where they were than accept a lie about themselves.

I'm also reminded of Shaykh Ali al-Timimi, imprisoned in the US for over 100 consecutive years due to false evidence given by individuals pressured by the state to turn on their teacher. He recounted his response to the government when he was asked to plead guilty:

> *We had asked the government, they had given me a choice last week to come in and confess to one crime and they would give me fourteen years in jail or face this indictment which carries, if I am found guilty – and we ask Allāh (azzawajal) to protect me from any evil – will face a life sentence. And of course, I could not sign or agree to something.*

> *I remember when I went to my parents, I was quite confused as to what to do – and my mother told me, she said, "Son, remember death only comes once in life." And my father who is 84/85 years old and is technically blind said to me, "Son I would prefer to see you die in prison and that you are keeping to your principles and to what you believe in rather than for you to sell your soul and to be rejected by yourself first and foremost and of course by your Lord."*

Ali al-Tamimi encapsulates much of the virtue of disobedience that I have been searching for. He finds the heart and the strength to place truth and integrity before all else, including the threat of prison – in that sense – he is the descendent of the Prophet Joseph, of Martin Luther King Jr and the many others who placed themselves in the line of danger for the sake of remaining virtuous. Ali al-Tamimi closes his speech by quoting one of my favourite sayings of Ibn Taymiyya. It is a saying that completely neutralises the power of coercion the state might bring to bear, for it places the individual above the most extreme harm that could be caused:

> *What can my enemies do to me? My Garden is in my heart; wherever I go, it goes with me. My imprisonment is solitary (worship of God)! My death is martyrdom! My banishment is a journey (across God's earth ...)[cxcv]*

The truth is one thing, but speaking it is another – to actually vocalise in the appropriate place and at the appropriate time the words that must be spoken is much more difficult to do than we can imagine. The nihilists, the ones who resort to violence for they cannot find any other form of expression, actually haven't understood their own fight. They feel that by attacking innocent people in the west, they will somehow be considered among the ranks of the mujahideen. But surely this was actually an easier way out for them? It did not require any sacrifice except for their own lives, no consequences except those that they will face in the afterlife. This is how I finally came to understand the tradition of the Prophet when he said:

> *"What is the most virtuous struggle (jihad)?" The Prophet said, "A word of truth in front of a tyrannical ruler."[cxcvi]*

Unlike the fighter, the truth-speaker has no weapons except his heart and his tongue. He has no armour to defend himself except the protection that Allāh grants him. So now I understand, that the one who speaks truth to power has the highest state as a mujahid before Allāh, because it takes courage to speak the truth in an environment where you are alone and small compared to the machinery of the state. I also now understand that when Allāh describes in the Qur'ān the status of the most righteous, the group that immediately follows in the order of righteousness after the prophets are the siddiqeen the truth-speakers, even before the martyrs and the pious:

> "And he who obeys Allāh and the Prophet, he will be with those whom Allāh has favoured-the prophets, the siddiqeen (truthfuls), the shuhada (martyrs) and the saliheen (pious). And what good companions they are"[cxcvii]

Piety will get you far, but it cannot compare to the one who is willing to speak the truth on their own – these are the 'disobedient' heroes that we should take as our example when faced with injustice. The siddiqeen, are found to be virtuous in all their characteristics, but especially so in truth. So I come to the person who I think is perhaps my favourite modern day hero of all. Do not get me wrong, Muhammad Rabbani is a hero in a way that I cannot even imagine to be, but he has an entire team behind him, backing him, giving him the support he needs. The person I am thinking of however, is Suriyah Bi. She took on the entirety of the establishment by herself, when law firms would not assist, when NGOs would not take her seriously, when unions failed her, and she won.

In September 2015, Suriyah Bi was dismissed from her post as a teaching assistant at the Heartlands Academy in Birmingham after she refused to show a video that was rated 18 to children who were 11-years-old. The video contained graphic images of the World Trade Centre attacks in 2001, and Bi took the decision not to show this video to the children in order to protect them. After being sacked from her position, Bi took the school to court and represented herself after being told that no law firm would take her case. Eventually she was vindicated by a tribunal.[cxcviii]

The case of Suriyah Bi might not seem as significant as other cases, such as those that I work on at Guantanamo Bay, or Philando Castile or indeed Muhammad Rabbani – but for me Bi represents something much more than any of them. It is the fact that she was willing and able to become the agent of her own success, to speak her truth and to not allow little details like not having a law degree to stop her from representing herself. She spoke truth to power, on her own, and she won. This is what it means to be virtuous in your disobedience.

In the chapter of the Quran quoted at the beginning of this book, Allāh swears by the fading light, that the whole of mankind is at loss (both Muslim and non-Muslim). Except for one group. A group that is described as having specific characteristics of belief and good deeds. However there are two other characteristics that are identified, and they are of those who enjoin truth and enjoin patience. The juxtaposition is an important one to reflect on. It is actually easy to speak the truth once. The heart actually allows for it as the human condition is one that our inclination is to say what is true and right. What is much more difficult, is that when the words of truth are released and find the oxygen of the air, they become real to those the truth is directed at. In that moment, the system emerges and attempts to destroy the truth, or destroy the individual. So the other virtue that the truth-speaker needs is patience, for it is one thing being truthful, it is entirely another to have patience on that truth.

I pray that we are all given the strength to be truth-speakers, and are among those who have the patience to bear its weight, until justice prevails. Amin.

Prayer Against Collaboration

The Prophetic tradition teaches the Muslim, that du'a (prayer) is the weapon of the believer. So, in light of the virtue of disobedience, I end by sharing this prayer written by Ibn al-Qayyim al-Jawziyya against collaborators and despots.

Asim Qureshi

I seek God's protection from those who lack knowledge and have sold their religion. They are insolent in their ignorance and use all their capabilities to harm Your servants. Due to their ignorance, such people consider benevolence to be evil, the Sunna [of the Prophet] to be blameworthy innovation in the religion, and good tradition to be strange. Due to their injustice, they recompense a good deed with evil and one evil with ten. They also disregard the rights of others and despise people, so that they may attain their false desires and pleasures. They do not acknowledge what is good except that which accords to their wishes, nor do they renounce what is abominable unless their desires oppose it. They act arrogantly with their loyal supporters (awliya) of the Messenger and they quicken to sit amongst those who are astray and ignorant. They may think that [in knowledge] they are the foremost, but God, His Messenger and the believers consider them to be cut off from the Prophet's inheritance.[cxcix]

Acknowledgments

All praise and thanks are due to Allāh alone, the Nourisher, the Creator, the Sustainer. Without Him, nothing I have done could be possible in any way.

As the narration of the Prophet informs us, the one who has not thanked the creation, has not thanked Allāh. With that in mind, before anyone else, I would like to recognise the contribution of my wife and children to this book, but in fact to all of my work. It is often all too natural to see the end product of something, without bringing into sharper focus all of the sacrifices that were made on the part of others. Having time to read and think is no pressure on me; it was in fact a joy. However, it always comes at a cost, in particular to my wife Samira Ahmed, who has consistently given me the support and freedom to do what I need – she is the spine of my efforts. My children, Haytham, Aadam and Sulayman, continue to show me love despite the long absences when I travel for work or hole myself up in my study – their affection despite it all, is a motivation for me. I continually pray, that they will be the first beneficiaries in our fight for justice.

My parents Abu and Ammi, siblings and their families. My mother-in-law, who I also call Ammi, my wife's siblings and their families. They are the example of the support network anyone fighting for justice needs. When I was going through the most difficult period of vilification in the media, and they were dragged into the media frenzy as collateral damage, they stood behind me and urged me to carry on. No seeker of justice could ever ask for anything more, than to know those you love and respect most in this world, will always support you.

To the entire team at CAGE, to the survivors and to

the families of those survivors. You are the lifeblood of my thinking. The team at CAGE, and all the other activists out there who support our work – you inspire me daily to be more principled, more just, more brave in my response to oppression, as you exemplify those characteristics. The survivors and their families – you are not victims – you are the conscience of our movement. Within each of you resides the authority to demand more from all of us, and your example remains as a mathematical constant within our equations of resistance.

To one group of people in particular, whose loss last year was of a degree that it is impossible to quantify. I miss Scharlette all the time, and can only imagine who hard it has been for all of you. I'm glad we have one another though and I cannot think of a better group of people to stand alongside as we seek justice together.

For those who supported the crowd-funding, this book would literally not have been possible without you. In that vein, my gratitude also goes to Suhaiymah Manzoor-Khan, who read my words and translated them into a verse that was so moving and powerful, that I wondered if my book now did justice to her poem.

Finally my thanks to James Patrick, Stephen Colgrave, and Peter Jukes from ByLine Books and ByLine Media – working with you all was a great example of how coming together is easier than it is sometimes made out to be. Thank you for believing in this book and supporting it throughout the process.

To the seekers of justice. I pray that we come together, and find solutions to the evils we see. Without one another, we can only fulfil our individual obligations to the oppressed and to our creator, but together, we can change the world.

Bibliography and Further Reading

Abdel Aziz B. (2016) The Queue. Melville House

Abdel Haleem M. (2008) The Qur'ān. Oxford World's Classics

Abdel Haleem M. & Badawi E.M. (2007) Arabic-English Dictionary of Qur'ānic Usage. Brill

Achebe C. (2006) Things Fall Apart. Penguin Classics.

Agamben G. (2005) State of Exception. University of Chicago Press

al-Ghazali Z. (1994) Return of the Pharaoh: Memoir in Nasir's Prison. The Islamic Foundation

al-Sha'rānī AW. (2017) Advice for Callow Jurists and Gullible Mendicants on Befriending Emirs. Yale University Press

Alderman N (2017) The Power. Penguin Random House.

Alexander M. (2012) The New Jim Crow. The New Press

Alyan H. (2017) Salt Houses. Houghton Mifflin Harcourt

Angelou M. (1997) I know why the caged bird sings. Random House. iBooks edition.

Anjum O. (2014) Politics, Law and Community in Islamic Thought: The Taymiyyan Moment. Cambridge University Press

Arendt H. (2006) Eichmann in Jerusalem: A Report on the Banality of Evil. Penguin Classics

Asimov I. (2013) I, Robot. Harper Voyager

Atwood M. (1996) The Handmaid's Tale. Vintage

Avraham R. (2014) Ottoman Empire: A Safe Haven for Jewish Refugees. Jerusalem Online

Baldwin J. (1990) The Fire Next Time: My Dungeon Shook; Dawn at the Cross. Penguin Classics

--- (2017) I Am Not Your Negro. Penguin Classics

Ballard J.G. (2014) High-Rise. Fourth Estate

Barrell R. (2015) Trevor Noah's Appearance On 'The John Bishop Show' Has Us Ready For 'The Daily Show'. Huffington Post

Barrett R (2013) Sensory Experience and the Women Martyrs of Najran. Journal of Early Christian Studies.

Biko S (1987) I Write What I Like. Heinemann

Boff C and Boff L (1987) Introducing Liberation Theology. Orbis Books

Bonilla-Silva E. (2014)Racism without Racists: Color-Blind Racism and the Persistence of Racial. Rowman & Littlefield Publishers.

Bracchi P. & Lemanski D. (2015) A very privileged apologist

for evil: An heiress wife. A £700k Surrey home. How the public school educated 'human rights' champion who praised Jihadi John lives the good life in the country he's trying to destroy. Daily Mail

Bradbury R (2008) Fahrenheit 451. Harper Voyager.

Brown J.A.C. (2016) Is there Justice Outside of God's Law? School of Oriental and African Studies. YouTube.

Bulman M (2017) Muslim children as young as nine branded terrorists in wake of recent terror attacks, reveals Childline. The Independent

Burgess A (1962) A Clockwork Orange. William Heinemann.

Butler O. (1993) Parable of the Sower. Headline Publishing Group. iBooks edition.

CAGE (2015) External Review Report into CAGE's handling of the Mohammed Emwazi Affair. CAGE

Cameron D (2011) PM's speech at Munich Security Conference. HM Government

Card OS (2011) Ender's Game. Orbit

Carr M. (2010) Blood and Faith: The Purging of Muslim Spain. Hurst & Co Publishers

Cemil A (2017) The Idea of the Muslim World: A Global Intellectual History. Harvard University Press

Chamayou G. (2015) Drone Theory. Penguin

Chammah M (2017) Scharlette Holdman, a Force for the Defense on Death Row, Dies at 70. New York Times

Choudhury T and Fenwick H (2011) The impact of counter-terrorism measures on Muslim communities. Equality and Human Rights Commission. Research Report 72.

Coates T-N. (2015) Between the World and Me. Text Publishing Company

Collins S (2008) The Hunger Games. Scholastic.

--- (2009) Catching Fire. Scholastic.

--- (2010) Mockingjay. Scholastic.

Cox B (2017) Jo Cox: More in Common. Two Roads

Davis A. (2016) Freedom Is a Constant Struggle : Ferguson, Palestine, and the Foundations of a Movement. Haymarket Books

de la Boetie E. (1975) The Politics of Obedience: The Discourse of Voluntary Servitude. The Mises Institute.

Dempsey N, Allen G and Politowski B (2017) Terrorism in Great Britain: the statistics. Commons Briefing Papers. Houses of Parliament.

Dick PK (2003) The Three Stigmata of Palmer Eldritch. Gollancz

--- (2015) The Man in the High Castle. Penguin Classics

Dodd V (2011) Terrorism Act: 'They asked me to keep an eye on the Muslim community'. The Guardian

Douglass F (2009) Narrative of the Life of Frederick Douglass. Oxford World Classics

Drury S. (2006) Political Ideas of Leo Strauss. Palgrave Macmillan.

Du Bois WEB (2007) The Souls of Black Folk. Oxford World Classics

Eddo-Lodge R (2017) Why I'm No Longer Talking to White People About Race. Bloomsbury Circus

Errachidi A. (2014) The General: The ordinary man who challenged Guantanamo. Vintage

Fanon F (2008) Black Skin White Masks. Pluto Press

Farris SR (2017) In the Name of Women's Rights. The Rise of Femonationalism. Duke University Press

Forman J (2017) Locking Up Our Own. Farrar

Foucault M (1991) Discipline and Punish: The Birth of the Prison. Penguin

Fulton S & Martin T (2017) Rest in Power: The Enduring Life of Trayvon Martin. Jacaranda Books

Gerges F. (1999) America and Political Islam: Clash of Cultures or Clash of Interests. Cambridge University Press

---- (2011) The irresistible rise of the Muslim Brothers. The NewStatesman

Gibson W (2016) Neuromancer. Gollancz

Guevara E.C. (2008) Guerilla Warfare. BN Publishing

Hallaq W.B. (2009) Shari'a – Theory, Practice, Transformations. Cambridge University Press

Hamid M (2017) Exit West. Riverhead Books.

Hanley L. (2017) Look at Grenfell Tower and see the terrible price of Britain's inequality. The Guardian

Herbert F (2007) Dune. Gollancz

Herman J. (2015) Trauma and Recovery: The aftermath of violence – from domestic abuse to political terror. Basic Books

Hill A (1998) Speaking Truth to Power. Anchor Books

Howey H. (2013) Wool. Arrow

--- (2013) Shift. Arrow

--- (2014) Dust. Arrow.

Hussin IR (2016) The Politics of Islamic Law: Local Elites, Colonial Authority and the Making of the Muslim State. University of Chicago Press

Huxley A (2007) Brave New World. Vintage

Ibn Abbas. Tanwir al-Miqbas min Tafsir ibn Abbas. Royal Aal al-Bayt Institute for Islamic Thought

Ibn al-Qayyim al-Jawziyya. (2017) On Knowledge. Islamic Text Society

Institute for Economics & Peace (2016) Global Terrorism Index. START.

Ishiguro K (2010) Never Let Me Go. Faber & Faber

Johnson E.M. (2017) Justine Damond shooting: Minneapolis police chief resigns amid protests over unarmed Australian woman's killing. The Independent

Kafka F (2015) The Trial. Penguin Classics

Karnani A (2007) Doing Well by Doing Good: Case Study: 'Fair & Lovely' Whitening Cream. Michigan Ross School of Business. SMJ 07-6615 rev.

Kennedy M (2007) Enough, says Amis, in Eagleton feud. The Guardian

King ML (2000) The Autobiography of Martin Luther King Jr. Abacus

King S (2003) The Gunslinger. Viking.

Klein N. (2017) No Is Not Enough: Defeating the New Shock Politics. Allen Lane

Klug B. (2015) Fawlty Logic: The Cracks in Cameron's 2011 Munich Speech. ReOrient

Kundapara S. (2013) Mir Sadik – Symbol of betrayal in our history. Samudaya Kundapura blog

Kundnani A. (2014) The Muslims are Coming. Verso Books

Lasher M. (2016) Read the Full Transcript of Jesse Williams' Powerful Speech on Race at the BET Awards. TIME

Lewis S (2017) It Can't Happen Here. Penguin Modern Classics

Levi P (1991) If This is a Man/The Truce. Abacus

Lowery W (2017) They Can't Kill Us All. Penguin

Mandela N (1995) Long Walk to Freedom. Abacus

Massoumi N et al (2017) What is Islamophobia? Racism, Social Movements and the State. Pluto Press

McCarthy C (2009) The Road. Picador

McMullen T (2015) What does the panopticon mean in the age of digital surveillance? The Guardian.

Mishra P (2013) From the Ruins of Empire: The Revolt Against the West and the Remaking of Asia. Penguin

---- (2014) The Western Model is Broken. The Guardian

Morris W (2012) News from Nowhere or an Epoch of Rest. CreateSpace Independent Publishing Platform

Morsi Y (2017) Radical Skin Moderate Masks: De-radicalising the Muslim and Racism in Post-racial Societies. Rowman & Littlefield International

Mortimer C. (2016) Eight-year-old boy questioned after teachers mistake t-shirt slogan for Isis propaganda. The Independent

Mounzer L. (2016) War in Translation: Giving Voice to the Women of Syria. Literary Hub.

Nolan WF (2015) Logan's Run. Vintage Books

Norton A (2013) On the Muslim Question. Princeton University Press

Pappe I. (2007) The Ethnic Cleansing of Palestine. Oneworld Publications

Qureshi A (2016) EXCLUSIVE: CAGE's Asim Qureshi reviews explosive new book on 'Jihadi John'. Middle East Eye

Ragazzi F. (2015) Suspect community or suspect category? The impact of counter-terrorism as 'policed multiculturalism'. Journal of Ethnic and Migration Studies.Vol.42 Issue.5

Rees L. (2017) The Holocaust: A New History. Viking

Roth P. (2005) The Plot Against America. Vintage

Sageman M. (2016) Misunderstanding Terrorism. University of Pennsylvania Press

Said E.W. (2003) Orientalism. Penguin

Sanchez R. (2014) Gerry Conlon: Tormented in life, remembered in death. The Telegraph

Saramago J. (2013) Blindness. Vintage Classics

Schafft G.E. (2007) From Racism to Genocide: Anthropology in the Third Reich. University of Illinois Press

Shaheen F. (2016) I was held after reading a book on a plane – we need to rethink our terror laws. The Guardian

Shakur A. (2014) Assata: An Autobiography. Zed Books

Shakur T.A. (1992) Changes. Interscope Records

Shukla N (2016) The Good Immigrant. Ubound. iBooks edition

Silverberg R. (1977) Shadrach in the Furnace. Readers Union. First Thus edition

Smith P. (2017) A Whistleblower Who Was Fired For Objecting To Kids Watching A Video Of 9/11 Has Won A Legal Victory. BuzzFeed

Snyder T. (2017) On Tyranny: Twenty Lessons from the Twentieth Century. Bodley Head.

Tanpinar A.H. (2014) The Time Regulation Institute. Penguin Modern Classics

Taylor D. (2017) Met police investigating Muslim man's wrongful arrest over terrorism. The Guardian

Thoreau H.D. (2017) On the Duty of Civil Disobedience. CreateSpace Independent Publishing Platform

Tharoor S. (2017) Inglorious Empire. Hurst & Co Publishers

Warren DH (2017) Cleansing the nation of the "dogs of hell": 'Ali Jum'a's nationalist legal reasoning in support of the 2013 Egyptian coup and its bloody aftermath. Int. J. Middle East Stud. 49 (2017)

Warsi S (2017) The Enemy Within: A Tale of Muslim Britain. Allen Lane

Washington BT (2015) Up From Slavery. CreatSpace Independent Publishing Platform

William F (2015) Logan's Run. Vintage

X M (2007) The Autobiography of Malcolm X. Penguin

Yizhar S. (2011) Khirbet Khizeh. Granta Books.

Zamoyski A. (2015) Phantom Terror: The Threat of Revolution and the Repression of Liberty 1789–1848. William Collins iIbn al-Qayyim al-Jawziyya. (2017) *On Knowledge*. Islamic Text Society, pp.270-271

iiAbdel Haleem M.A.S (2010) *The Qur'ān*, Oxford World Classics, p.435

iiiWhite M (2015) *Shaker Aamer: a 'very bad man' or simply wronged?* The Guardian.

ivAlexander M. (2012) The New Jim Crow. The New Press. p.180

vHHUGS (accessed 27.06.2017) *Meet Ali & Aisha*
http://hhugs.org.uk/meet-ali-aisha/560

viAgamben G (2005) State of Exception. University of Chicago Press

viiDempsey N, Allen G and Politowski B (2017) Terrorism in Great Britain: the statistics. Commons Briefing Papers. Houses of Parliament.

viiiBulman M (2017) Muslim children as young as nine branded terrorists in wake of recent terror attacks, reveals Childline. The Independent

ixKlug B. (2015) *Fawlty Logic: The Cracks in Cameron's 2011 Munich Speech*. ReOrient

xKloisin A. et al (2017) *Transgenerational transmission of environmental information in C. elegans* . Science. Vol. 356, Issue 6335, p.323

xiAlyan H. (2017) *Salt Houses*. Houghton Mifflin Harcourt. p.145

xiiYizhar S. (2011) *Khirbet Khizeh*. Granta Books. pp.104-105

xiiiSanchez R (2014) Gerry Conlon: Tormented in life, remembered in death. The Telegraph

xivChamayou G. (2015) Drone Theory. Penguin. p.71

xvAbdel Haleem M.A.S (2010) *The Qur'ān*, Oxford World Classics, p.252, 29:2-3

xviBoff C and Boff L (1987) Introducing Liberation Theology. Orbis Books. p.34

xviiSnyder T (2017) On Tyranny: Twenty Lessons from the Twentieth Century. Bodley Head.

xviiiAbdel Haleem M.A.S (2010) *The Qur'ān*, Oxford World Classics, p.244 28:3-5

xixLevi P (1991) *If This is a Man/The Truce*. Abacus

xxFoucault M (1991) *Discipline and Punish: The Birth of the Prison*. Penguin

xxiSchafft G.E. (2007) *From Racism to Genocide: Anthropology in the Third Reich*. University of Illinois Press

xxiiPappe I. (2007) *The Ethnic Cleansing of Palestine*. Oneworld Publications

xxiiiCarr M. (2010) *Blood and Faith: The Purging of Muslim Spain*. Hurst & Co Publishers

xxivAvraham R. (2014) *Ottoman Empire: A Safe Haven for Jewish Refugees*. Jerusalem Online

xxvHallaq W.B. (2009) *Shari'a – Theory, Practice, Transformations*. Cambridge University Press. pp.377–78

xxviHallaq W.B. (2009) *Shari'a – Theory, Practice, Transformations*. Cambridge University Press. pp.377–78

xxviiBiko S (1987) I Write What I Like. Heinemann. p.36

xxviiiChamayou G. (2015) Drone Theory. Penguin

xxixCarr M. (2010) *Blood and Faith: The Purging of Muslim Spain*. Hurst & Co Publishers

xxxCarr M. (2010) *Blood and Faith: The Purging of Muslim Spain*. Hurst & Co Publishers xxxiZamoyski A. (2015) *Phantom Terror: The Threat of Revolution and the Repression of Liberty 1789–1848*. William Collins

xxxiiSageman M. (2016) *Misunderstanding Terrorism.* University of Pennsylvania Press, p.56

xxxiiiBiko S (1987) I Write What I Like. Heinemann. pp.76-77

xxxivAbdel Haleem M.A.S (2010) *The Qur'ān*, Oxford World Classics, p.24, 2:217

xxxvKing ML (2000) The Autobiography of Martin Luther King Jr. Abacus. p.338

xxxviSaid E.W. (2003) *Orientalism.* Penguin. p.xvi

xxxviiKing ML (2000) The Autobiography of Martin Luther King Jr. Abacus. p.361

xxxviiiFoucault M (1991) Discipline and Punish: The Birth of the Prison. Penguin. p.60

xxxixMounzer L. (2016) War in Translation: Giving Voice to the Women of Syria. Literary Hub.

xlAbdel Haleem M.A.S (2010) *The Qur'ān*, Oxford World Classics, p.81, 6:19

xlial-Bukhari, *The Book of Compulsion*, 12/315,316

xliiMuslim, *The Book of Piety*, 130

xliiiBarrett R (2013) *Sensory Experience and the Women Martyrs of Najran*. Journal of Early Christian Studies.

xlivBarrett R (2013) *Sensory Experience and the Women Martyrs of Najran*. Journal of Early Christian Studies. p.98

xlvAbdel Haleem M.A.S (2010) *The Qur'ān*, Oxford World Classics, p.416, 85:1-9

xlviRees L. (2017) *The Holocaust: A New History*. Viking

xlviiAbdel Haleem M.A.S (2010) *The Qur'ān*, Oxford World Classics, p.338, 49:13

xlviiiKarnani A (2007) *Doing Well by Doing Good: Case Study: 'Fair & Lovely' Whitening Cream*. Michigan Ross School of Business. SMJ 07-6615 rev. p.5

xlixKarnani A (2007) *Doing Well by Doing Good: Case Study: 'Fair & Lovely' Whitening Cream*. Michigan Ross School of Business. SMJ 07-6615 rev. p.6

l Shakur A. (2014) Assata: An Autobiography. Zed Books. p.43

liEddo-Lodge R. (2017) Why I'm No Longer Talking to White People About Race. Bloomsbury Publishing

liiEddo-Lodge R. (2017) Why I'm No Longer Talking to White People About Race. Bloomsbury Publishing

liiiInstitute for Economics & Peace (2016) Global Terrorism Index. START.

livAbdel Haleem M.A.S (2010) *The Qur'ān*, Oxford World Classics, p.14, 2:124

lvMuslim. *Sahih*. 2586

lviAnjum O. (2014) *Politics, Law and Community in Islamic Thought: The Taymiyyan Moment*. Cambridge University Press

lviiSayyid S. (2014) *Recalling the Caliphate: Decolonization and World Order*. Hurst & Co Publishers

lviiiKhan S. (2016) *The Battle for British Islam: Reclaiming Muslim Identity from Extremism*. Saqi Books.

lixGove M. (2006) Celcius 7/7. Weidenfeld & Nicolson

lxBrown J.A.C. (2016) *Is there Justice Outside of God's Law?* School of Oriental and African Studies. YouTube.

lxiLocke J. (2010) *Second Treatise on Government*. Createspace Independent Publishing Platform

lxiiAnjum O. (2014) *Politics, Law and Community in Islamic Thought: The Taymiyyan Moment*. Cambridge University Press

lxiiiQureshi A (2006) O Brother Where Art Thou? Islam21c

lxivQureshi A (2006) O Brother Where Art Thou? Islam21c

lxvFarris SR (2017) In the Name of Women's Rights. The Rise of Femonationalism. Duke University Press. p.116

lxviMarqusee M (2005) *Redemption Song: Muhammad Ali and the Spirit of the Sixties*. Verso Books

lxviiMarqusee M (2005) *Redemption Song: Muhammad Ali and the Spirit of the Sixties*. Verso Books

lxviiiDu Bois WEB (2007) The Souls of Black Folk. Oxford World Classics. p.38

lxixDu Bois WEB (2007) The Souls of Black Folk. Oxford World Classics. p.44

lxxBeary D. (2014) *Pro Wrestling Is Fake, but Its Race Problem Isn't*. The Atlantic

lxxiShakur T.A. (1992) *Changes*. Interscope Records

lxxiiKlein N. (2017) *No Is Not Enough: Defeating the New Shock Politics*. Allen Lane. p.56

lxxiiiShakur A. (2014) Assata: An Autobiography. Zed Books. p.29

lxxivKlein N. (2017) *No Is Not Enough: Defeating the New Shock Politics*. Allen Lane. pp.9-10

lxxvEddo-Lodge R. (2017) Why I'm No Longer Talking to White People About Race. Bloomsbury Publishing

lxxviDu Bois WEB (2007) The Souls of Black Folk. Oxford World Classics. p.119

lxxviiSaid E.W. (2003) *Orientalism*. Penguin. p.xv

lxxviiiHanley L (2017) Look at Grenfell Tower and see the terrible price of Britain's inequality. The Guardian

lxxixBBC News (2017) London fire: A visual guide to what happened at Grenfell Tower. BBC

lxxxAssociated Press (2017) *Police officer who shot dead Philando Castile acquitted of all charges*. The Guardian

lxxxiJohnson E.M. (2017) *Justine Damond shooting: Minneapolis police chief resigns amid protests over unarmed Australian woman's killing*. The Independent

lxxxiiBonilla-Silva, E. (2014)Racism without Racists: Color-Blind Racism and the Persistence of Racial. Rowman & Littlefield Publishers. p.3-4

lxxxiiiFulton S. & Martin T. (2017) *Rest in Power: The Enduring Life of Trayvon Martin*. Jacaranda Books

lxxxivOffice for Security and Counter-Terrorism (2012) *Channel Vulnerability Assessment Framework*. Home Office. HM Government

lxxxvArdent H. (2006) Eichmann in Jerusalem. Penguin Classics.

lxxxviShaheen F. (2016) *I was held after reading a book on a plane – we need to rethink our terror laws*. The Guardian

lxxxvii Taylor D. (2017) *Met police investigating Muslim man's wrongful arrest over terrorism*. The Guardian lxxxviiiMassoumi N et al (2017) What is Islamophobia? Racism, Social Movements and the State. Pluto Press

lxxxixBaldwin J. (2017) I Am Not Your Negro. Penguin Classics. p.98

xcLasher M. (2016) *Read the Full Transcript of Jesse Williams' Powerful Speech on Race at the BET Awards.* TIME

xciIbn Kathir, Tafsir al-Qur'ān al- 'Adhim, 40:28

xciiIbn Abbas, Tanwir al-Miqbas min Tafsir ibn Abbas, Royal Aal al-Bayt Institute for Islamic Thought, Amman, Jordan, 2008, 40:28

xciiiQutb S, In the Shade of the Qur'ān, The Islamic Foundation, tr. Adil Salahi, vol.XV, p.36

xcivl Haleem M.A.S (2010) *The Qur'ān*, Oxford World Classics, p.304, 40:46-48

xcv Drury S. (2006) Political Ideas of Leo Strauss. Palgrave Macmillan. p.xxiv

xcviFanon F (2008) Black Skin White Masks. Pluto Press

xcviiX M. (1963) *The Race Problem*. African Students Association and NAACP Campus Chapter. Michigan State University

xcviiiDouglass F (2009) Narrative of the Life of Frederick Douglass. Oxford World Classics. p.23

xcixLevi P (1991) *If This is a Man/The Truce*. Abacus

cBiko S (1987) I Write What I Like. Heinemann. p.37

ciVirtual Shtetl. (2010) *Anniversary of the liquidation of the Warsaw Ghetto.*

ciiRees L. (2017) *The Holocaust: A New History*. Viking

ciiiDu Bois WEB (2007) The Souls of Black Folk. Oxford World Classics. p.135

civCoates T-N. (2015) *Between the World and Me*. Text Publishing Company

cvForman J (2017) Locking Up Our Own. Farrar. p.9

cviForman J (2017) Locking Up Our Own. Farrar. p.108

cviiBracchi P. & Lemanski D. (2015) *A very privileged apologist for evil: An heiress wife. A £700k Surrey home. How the public school educated 'human rights' champion who praised Jihadi John lives the good life in the country he's trying to destroy.* Daily Mail

cviiiMekhennet S. (2017) *I Was Told To Come Alone: My Journey Behind The Lines of Jihad*. Virago

cixBracchi P. & Lemanski D. (2015) *A very privileged apologist for evil: An heiress wife. A £700k Surrey home. How the public school educated 'human rights' champion who praised Jihadi John lives the good life in the country he's trying to destroy.* Daily Mail

cxHaleem M.A.S (2010) *The Qur'ān*, Oxford World Classics, p.232, 26:16-18

cxiHaleem M.A.S (2010) *The Qur'ān*, Oxford World Classics, p.233, 26:22

cxiide la Boetie E. (1975) *The Politics of Obedience: The Discourse of Voluntary Servitude*. The Mises Institute.

cxiiiQutb S. (2004) *In the Shade of the Quran*. Islamic Foundation. Vol.18.

cxivde la Boetie E. (1975) *The Politics of Obedience: The Discourse of Voluntary Servitude*. The Mises Institute.

cxvBarrell R. (2015) *Trevor Noah's Appearance On 'The John Bishop Show' Has Us Ready For 'The Daily Show'.* Huffington Post

cxvi Kundapara S. (2013) Mir Sadik – Symbol of betrayal in our history. Samudaya Kundapura blog cxviiTharoor S. (2017) *Inglorious Empire.* Hurst & Co Publishers

cxviiiMishra P. (2014) *The Western Model is Broken.* The Guardian

cxixHussin I.R. (2016) The Politics of Islamic Law: Local Elites, Colonial Authority, and the Making of the Muslim State. University of Chicago Press

cxxMishra P (2013) *From the Ruins of Empire: The Revolt Against the West and the Remaking of Asia.* Penguin

cxxial-Sha'rānī AW. (2017) *Advice for Callow Jurists and Gullible Mendicants on Befriending Emirs.* Yale University Press

cxxiial-Sha'rānī AW. (2017) *Advice for Callow Jurists and Gullible Mendicants on Befriending Emirs.* Yale University Press

cxxiiial-Sha'rānī AW. (2017) *Advice for Callow Jurists and Gullible Mendicants on Befriending Emirs.* Yale University Press

cxxivAnjum O. (2014) *Politics, Law and Community in Islamic Thought: The Taymiyyan Moment.* Cambridge University Press

cxxvWarren DH (2017) *Cleansing the nation of the "dogs of hell": 'Ali Jum'a's nationalist legal reasoning in support of the 2013 Egyptian coup and its bloody aftermath.* Int. J. Middle East Stud. 49 (2017). p.457

cxxvial-Ghazali Z. (1994) *Return of the Pharaoh: Memoir in Nasir's Prison.* The Islamic Foundation. pp.13-14

cxxviiRagazzi F. (2015) Suspect community or suspect category? The impact of counter-terrorism as 'policed multiculturalism'. Journal of Ethnic and Migration Studies.Vol.42 Issue.5

cxxviiiKundnani A. (2014) *The Muslims are Coming.* Verso Books

cxxixBoff C and Boff L (1987) Introducing Liberation Theology. Orbis Books. p.86

cxxxKundnani A. (2014) *The Muslims are Coming.* Verso Books

cxxxide la Boetie E. (1975) *The Politics of Obedience: The Discourse of Voluntary Servitude.* The Mises Institute.

cxxxiiLasher M. (2016) *Read the Full Transcript of Jesse Williams' Powerful Speech on Race at the BET Awards.* TIME

cxxxiiiMassoumi N et al (2017) What is Islamophobia? Racism, Social Movements and the State. Pluto Press

cxxxivSnyder T (2017) On Tyranny: Twenty Lessons from the Twentieth Century. Bodley Head.

cxxxvSnyder T (2017) On Tyranny: Twenty Lessons from the Twentieth Century. Bodley Head.

cxxxviKing M.L. (2013) *Letter From Birmingham Jail.* The Atlantic

cxxxviiX M. (1964) *Oxford Union Debate.*

cxxxviiiMorsi Y (2017) Radical Skin Moderate Masks: De-radicalising the Muslim and Racism in Post-racial Societies. Rowman & Littlefield International. p.38

cxxxixCameron D (2011) PM's speech at Munich Security Conference. HM Government

cxlTaneja P. (2014) *Army imam says British Muslims can be good soldiers.* BBC Asian Network

cxliLevi P (1991) *If This is a Man/The Truce.* Abacus

cxliiIbn al-Qayyim al-Jawziyya. (2017) *On Knowledge.* Islamic Text Society

cxliiiSnyder T (2017) On Tyranny: Twenty Lessons from the Twentieth Century. Bodley Head.

cxlivQureshi A (2015) *On Gangsta Rap and Jihadi Songs.* Media

Diversified

cxlvStuart H. (2017) *Islamist Terrorism: Analysis of Offences and Attacks in the UK (1998-2015)*. The Henry Jackson Society

cxlviSageman M. (2016) *Misunderstanding Terrorism*. University of Pennsylvania Press, p.?

cxlviiSageman M. (2016) *Misunderstanding Terrorism*. University of Pennsylvania Press, p.?

cxlviiiLewis B. (1990) *The Roots of Muslim Rage*. The Atlantic

cxlixSaid E.W. (2003) *Orientalism*. Penguin. Pp.318-319

clGerges F. (1999) *America and Political Islam: Clash of Cultures or Clash of Interests*. Cambridge University Press

cliBiko S (1987) I Write What I Like. Heinemann. pp.21-22

cliiKundnani A. (2016) *Islamophobia: lay ideology of US-led empire*. Kundnani.org

cliiiKennedy M (2007) *Enough, says Amis, in Eagleton feud*. The Guardian

clivTanpinar A.H. (2014) *The Time Regulation Institute*. Penguin Modern Classics. p.xviii

clvOffice of the Press Secretary (2017) *President Trump's Speech to the Arab Islamic American Summit*. The White House

clviKlug B. (2015) *Fawlty Logic: The Cracks in Cameron's 2011 Munich Speech*. ReOrient

clviiMounzer L. (2016) *War in Translation*. Lit Hub

clviiiKhalili L. (2012) *Time in the Shadows: Confinement and Counterinsurgencies*. Stanford University Press

clixRahman A. (2013) *Fear of a Brown Planet*. Genius

clxDouglass F (2009) Narrative of the Life of Frederick Douglass. Oxford World Classics. pp.38-39

clxiCoates T-N. (2015) *Between the World and Me*. Text Publishing Company

clxiiChammah M (2017) *Scharlette Holdman, a Force for the Defense on Death Row, Dies at 70*. New York Times

clxiiiX M. (1963) *Message to the Grass Roots*. Detroit

clxivBaldwin J. (1990) *The Fire Next Time: My Dungeon Shook; Dawn at the Cross*. Penguin Classics

clxvIbn Abbas, *Tanwir al-Miqbas min Tafsir Ibn Abbas*, Royal Aal al-Bayt Institute for Islamic Thought, Amman, Jordan, 2008, 4:75

clxvial-Jalalayn, *Tafsir*, Royal Aal al-Bayt Institute for Islamic Thought, Amman, Jordan, 2013, 4:75

clxviiAbdel Haleem M.A.S (2010) *The Qur'ān*, Oxford World Classics, 2010, p.57 4:75

clxviiiGuevara E.C. (2008) Guerilla Warfare. BN Publishing

clxixde la Boetie E. (1975) *The Politics of Obedience: The Discourse of Voluntary Servitude*. The Mises Institute.

clxxHerman J. (2015) Trauma and Recovery: The aftermath of violence – from domestic abuse to political terror. Basic Books

clxxiErrachidi A. (2014) *The General: The ordinary man who challenged Guantanamo*. Vintage

clxxiiDavis A. (2016) *Freedom Is a Constant Struggle : Ferguson, Palestine, and the Foundations of a Movement*. Haymarket Books

clxxiiiDavis A. (2016) *Freedom Is a Constant Struggle : Ferguson, Palestine, and the Foundations of a Movement*. Haymarket Books

clxxivIbn Kathir, Tafsir al-Qurʾān al- ʿAdhim, 8:42

clxxvQureshi A. (2016) *Interview with AAM*. CAGE

clxxviAngelou M. (1997) *I know why the caged bird sings*. Random House. iBooks edition. p.325

clxxviiNoah T. (2017) *The Truth about the Philando Castile Verdict*. The Daily Show

clxxviiiNoah T. (2017) *The Truth about the Philando Castile Verdict*. The Daily Show

clxxixQureshi A (2016) *EXCLUSIVE: CAGE's Asim Qureshi reviews explosive new book on 'Jihadi John'.* Middle East Eye

clxxxCAGE (2015) External Review Report into CAGE's handling of the Mohammed Emwazi Affair. CAGE

clxxxiMorsi Y (2017) Radical Skin, Moderate Masks. Rowman & Littlefield International. pp.44-45

clxxxiiDavis A. (2016) *Freedom Is a Constant Struggle : Ferguson, Palestine, and the Foundations of a Movement*. Haymarket Books

clxxxiiiMcMullen T (2015) *What does the panopticon mean in the age of digital surveillance?* The Guardian.

clxxxivChamayou G. (2015) Drone Theory. Penguin

clxxxvLiberty. *Schedule 7*. Counter-Terrorism. https://www.liberty-human-rights.org.uk/human-rights/countering-terrorism/schedule-7

clxxxviChoudhury T and Fenwick H (2011) *The impact of counter-terrorism measures on Muslim communities*. Equality and Human Rights Commission. Research Report 72.

clxxxviiShukla N (2016) *The Good Immigrant*. Unbound. iBooks edition. pp.313-314

clxxxviiiGreen S.J. (2017) *Hate-crime suspicions cloud death of Muslim teen in Lake Stevens*. The Seattle Times

clxxxixDodd V (2011) *Terrorism Act: 'They asked me to keep an eye on the Muslim community'.* The Guardian

cxcRabbani M. (2017) *'I am willing to go to prison for privacy for us all'.* Al Jazeera

cxciKing M.L. (2013) *Letter From Birmingham Jail*. The Atlantic

cxciiThoreau H.D. (2017) *On the Duty of Civil Disobedience*. CreateSpace Independent Publishing Platform

cxciiiHaleem M.A.S (2010) *The Qur'ān*, Oxford World Classics, p.147, 12:33

cxcivHaleem M.A.S (2010) *The Qur'ān*, Oxford World Classics, p.148, 12:50

cxcvAnjum O. (2014) *Politics, Law and Community in Islamic Thought: The Taymiyyan Moment*. Cambridge University Press

cxcviAhmad, *Musnad*, 1844

cxcviiHaleem M.A.S (2010) *The Qur'ān*, Oxford World Classics, p.57, 4:69

cxcviiiSmith P (2017) *A Whistleblower Who Was Fired For Objecting To Kids Watching A Video Of 9/11 Has Won A Legal Victory*. BuzzFeed

cxcixIbn al-Qayyim al-Jawziyya. (2017) *On Knowledge*. Islamic Text Society

Lightning Source UK Ltd.
Milton Keynes UK
UKHW03f2321180418
321314UK00002B/43/P